A Leader's Guide to Managing in Turbulent Times

Survival Strategies for Christian Colleges and Universities

Melissa Morriss-Olson

Coalition for Christian Colleges & Universities

© by the Coalition for Christian Colleges & Universities
ISBN: 0-9652730-0-8

Printed in the United States of America

As a professional association of academic institutions, the Coalition for Christian Colleges & Universities focuses on helping Christian colleges and universities better fulfill their mission to effectively integrate scholarship, faith, and service. The Coalition coordinates professional development opportunities for administrators and faculty, off-campus student programs, public advocacy for Christ-centered higher education, and cooperative efforts among member colleges and universities.

Founded in 1976 and incorporated in 1982, the Coalition has a membership of 90 four-year colleges and universities. Member institutions are the focus and core of the Coalition, but the association also involves a growing number of affiliated institutions of higher education in the United States and around the world.

The Coalition is a member of the Evangelical Council for Financial Accountability, the National Association of Independent Colleges and Universities, and the Christian Stewardship Association. The Coalition also holds associate membership in the Council of Independent Colleges.

Through the years, numerous foundations, businesses, and individuals have supported the Coalition and its programs, in addition to dues from member institutions and fees for various programs. The Coalition is a nonprofit, tax exempt organization under section 501(c)(3) of the IRS code. For additional information, please contact the Coalition for Christian Colleges & Universities at 329 Eighth Street NE, Washington, DC 20002-6158.

Telephone: (202) 546-8713
Fax: (202) 546-8913
E-mail: Coalition@cccu.org

Table of Contents

Tables and Figures iv

Foreword v

Preface vi

Acknowledgments vii

Chapter One
    Introduction and Overview of the Study...1

Chapter Two
    The Current Condition of the Christian College and University Sector....................15

Chapter Three
    A Framework for Understanding Institutional Resiliency 39

Chapter Four
    The Characteristics of Resilient Christian Colleges and Universities 59

Chapter Five
    Lessons for Institutional Leaders..77

Appendices
    Appendix A List of Participating Institutions 86
    Appendix B Strategic Management Survey 88
    Appendix C Operationalization of the Financial Condition Measures 110

References 114

Tables and Figures

Figure 1	Public and Nonpublic High School Graduates 1978 to 2008 (projected)	3
Figure 2	Public and Nonpublic High School Graduates by Region 1978 to 2008 (projected)	3
Figure 3	Categories of Approaches to Organizational Adaptation	41
Table 1	Institutions of Higher Education That Have Closed Their Doors 1960-61 to 1991-92	5
Table 2	Undergraduate Enrollment Change by Headcount by Group 1981 to 1991	17
Table 3	Enrollment Change by FTE by Group 1981 to 1991	17
Table 4	Change in Student Demographics by Group 1981 to 1991	19
Table 5	Change in Student Demographics by Group 1981 to 1991	19
Table 6	Graduate Enrollment Change by Headcount by Group 1981 to 1991	20
Table 7	Change in Programmatic Variables by Group	20
Table 8	Location of Schools by Region by Group	22
Table 9	Location of Coalition Schools by Environment and Location by Group	22
Table 10	Enrollment Change by Institutional Size by Group 1981 to 1991	23
Table 11	Freshman Headcount Change by Group 1981 to 1991	24
Table 12	Change in Freshman Enrollment Yields by Group 1981 to 1991	25
Table 13	Admissions Characteristics by Group	26
Table 14	Change in Student Demographics by Group 1981 to 1991	27
Table 15	Change in Student Demographics by Group 1981 to 1991	28
Table 16	Change in Financial Ratio: Unrestricted Funds Balance to Total Expenditures and Mandatory Transfers by Group 1981 to 1991	29
Table 17	Change in Financial Ratio: Net Revenues to Total Revenues by Group 1981 to 1991	31
Table 18	Change in Financial Ratio: Tuition and Fee Revenues to Total E & G Revenues by Group 1981 to 1991	31
Table 19	Change in Financial Ratio: Private Gifts and Grants to Total Expenditures and Mandatory Transfers by Group 1981 to 1991	32
Table 20	Change in Financial Ratio: Endowment Income to Total E & G Revenues by Group 1981 to 1991	32
Table 21	Change in Financial Ratio: Instructional Expenditures to Total E & G Revenues by Group 1981 to 1991	33
Table 22	Change in Financial Ratio: Total Assets to Total Liabilities by Group 1981 to 1991	34
Table 23	A Comparison of the Adaptive and Interpretive Models of Strategic Management	48
Table 24	Summary of Successful College Management Research Findings: Factors Influencing Institutional Resiliency and Decline	50
Table 25	Significant Forced Entry Regression Results of Weighted Index on the Selected Independent Variables	62
Table 26	Items Reflecting Commitment to Mission and Purpose	65
Table 27	Items Reflecting Opportunistic Stance	67
Table 28	Items Reflecting Effectiveness Orientation	68
Table 29	Items Reflecting Conservation and Resource Preservation Stance	69
Table 30	Items Reflecting Caring Campus Culture	70
Table 31	Items Reflecting Image Cultivation Efforts	72
Table 32	Comparison of Adaptive and Interpretive Strategy Usage for Improving, Stable and Declining Colleges	74

Foreword

Turbulent. Unpredictable. Lean. Competitive. Such words describe well the environment facing college and university leaders in recent years. These pressures present particular challenges for the leaders of our Christian liberal arts colleges and universities. It is telling that a number of higher education "experts" forecast the demise of as many as 400 colleges by the early 1990s, the most vulnerable being the "small, church-related, liberal arts colleges" (National Institute of Independent Colleges and Universities, 1980). This prediction is made credible by the fact that since 1960 over 300 institutions have closed their doors — including many church-related colleges. Indeed, never before has the task of shaping the future of Christian higher education demanded such concentration, perseverance, and skill.

Of the approximately 3,500 colleges and universities in the United States, only a small portion (20%) maintain some linkage to a specific church denomination or religious tradition. An even smaller sub-group are referred to as "Christ-centered," the 90 schools which comprise the Coalition for Christian Colleges & Universities. Of the approximately 15 million students enrolled in 1995 in American higher education, the Coalition schools are preparing about 150,000 men and women for future leadership roles in the body of Christ.

We believe that the need for Christian higher education in our society has never been greater. The Christian faith is at the heart of what a Christ-centered college or university is all about. These institutions provide students with a Christian worldview and the tools to live out their faith in all of life's arenas. In today's troubled times, the need is great for men and women who have experienced the Christian college difference.

Yet, the continued strength and viability of our Christian colleges and universities is not assured. Effective Christian college leadership in today's world requires, among other things, shrewd marketing skills, sophisticated development practices, solid management tools, an innovative mindset, keen insight and vision, and courage. The colleges and universities that will continue to thrive tomorrow are those that respond in focused ways to the challenges today.

My sincere hope is that this book will encourage, affirm, and enable campus leaders and managers to position their institutions for a strong future. This sourcebook is the first ever written specifically about successful Christian college management practices. It is grounded in the experiences of our most resilient Coalition institutions and provides a wealth of specific examples of how these schools are coping with hard economic times. Written by Dr. Melissa Morriss-Olson, vice president at North Park College, one of our member institutions, this book is must reading for Christian college administrators and trustees, as well as others concerned about the future of their institutions.

As you learn from the valuable examples and detail contained in the chapters that follow, please pray that God's wisdom will guide all who have been called to leadership in these special institutions.

Robert C. Andringa, President
Coalition for Christian Colleges & Universities
Washington, D.C.

Preface

Hardly a week goes by without yet another media account of a college or university "in crisis;" institutions on the brink of solvency, leaders under attack, and assaults from the public and elsewhere are but some of the gnawing issues capturing our attention these days. Clearly, American higher education is in the midst of difficult times. Such woes are hardly surprising to those familiar with the predictions of the "experts" beginning nearly thirty years ago and which ushered in this new era.

Christian colleges and universities are not immune from the pressures facing the broader higher education community. Indeed, Christ-centered institutions face unique challenges and constraints as they attempt to navigate through these turbulent waters. Because of their relative obscurity, limited resources, and narrow missions, such institutions have long been among those predicted to be most vulnerable to hard times. Surprisingly, no study has been conducted to date to find out how the Christian higher education sector is, in fact, holding up. It is to this end that this study was conducted.

This study was undertaken to find out how Christian liberal arts colleges and universities have been affected by recent hard times, how institutional leaders have risen to the challenges they have faced, what these responses mean to the broader Christian higher education community, and how one might account for those scattered instances of resiliency found across the sector.

I found enormous courage and great resilience among a number of the Christian colleges in this study. This book is about the lessons these institutions have learned from hard times, including what they learned about "what worked" on their campuses. Among the lessons learned by the participating institutions in this study are the following:

- The roots of resiliency and/or decline are multi-dimensional, complex, and deep.
- There is no finite prescription for resiliency; the experience of the most resilient institutions in this study suggest that the formula for success is unique to each institution. Most important is the overall mix of strategies, the general level of activity, and the cultural context within which the management approach is implemented.
- An effective response to hard economic times typically involves the institution at many levels: mission, structure, programs, strategy, and people.
- The most successful change effort happens simultaneously on many fronts. Because the pace of change is faster than ever before, institutions must get into the mode of continuous adaptation and improvement.
- Institutions can improve their conditions, change in enlightened ways, and build qualities of resilience into their organizational structures and mindsets.

This book is written for all who care about the future of Christian higher education including trustees, presidents, vice presidents, deans, department leaders, faculty, and leaders in the broader Christian higher education community. Chapter One provides an overview of the challenges facing all of higher education in recent years as well as the specific pressures confronting Christian higher education. Chapter One concludes with an overview of the study which serves as the basis for this book. Chapter Two seeks to answer two questions: 1) How have the Christian colleges and universities fared during the turbulent 1980s? 2) What is the current condition of the Christian college sector? In Chapter

Two, readers will find a wealth of enrollment and financial benchmark data by which to assess the current state of the sector as well as the health of their own institutions.

In Chapter Three, I review the literature and research on institutional resiliency to help the reader understand the various responses to adversity and the reasons for institutional demise and/or resiliency. While the literature base is wide-ranging in nature, three common themes are evident: 1) Both internal and external factors contribute to institutional performance; 2) Managers can act to successfully influence institutional outcomes, and 3) When facing decline, it is just as important to avoid the tendency to hunker down and respond conservatively as it is to avoid adopting a rampant incrementalistic approach — or an uncontrolled opportunistic stance. According to the research, the most effective approach includes a mix of pre-determined strategy and opportunistic groping so as to adapt successfully.

What are the qualities of Christian colleges and universities that have stronger prospects for the future? In Chapter Four, the characteristics which distinguish the most resilient institutions from the other colleges and universities in the study are described and discussed. Happily, the results suggest that Christian college leaders can act to influence the condition of their institutions. For example, the most resilient institutions are more likely to have strengthened academic standards, expanded their residential population, added new markets, increased enrollments on all levels, exhibited a stronger commitment to mission, made greater strides in enhancing the overall campus climate, engaged in a greater overall number of strategies, and adopted an opportunistic mode of operation. These findings provide the basis for Chapter Five which contains practical suggestions and recommendations for Christian college leaders.

Acknowledgments

I am grateful to the many people who have helped make this book possible. The publishing of this book resulted from the prompting of Dr. Karen Longman, Coalition for Christian Colleges & Universities (CCCU) vice president, and the encouragement and support of Dr. Bob Andringa, CCCU president.

A special word of thanks goes to Dr. Terry Williams, associate professor of educatioal leadership and policy studies at Loyola University Chicago. Professor Williams directed the dissertation upon which this book is based and provided invaluable feedback and guidance throughout the duration of the study.

I am most appreciative to the busy administrators at the 65 participating institutions who took the time to fill out my somewhat cumbersome, 25-page survey. The candor and insights of these professionals were truly profound.

So, too, I wish to acknowledge the assistance of several colleagues at North Park College. Dr. Nancy Arnesen, professor of English, carefully read each chapter draft and offered numerous helpful and insightful editorial suggestions. My assistant, Karey Lopez, provided valuable proofreading expertise and administrative support at numerous points along the way. Margaret Frisbie, director of publications, played a significant role in coordination of the publication and in working with the logistics of keeping the project moving. Del Shimandle, graphic designer, lent his considerable talent to the project in providing the lay-out and artistic design for the book.

I am deeply grateful to North Park's president, Dr. David Horner, for his ongoing encouragement and for the real-life laboratory which he has provided at North Park over the past nine years. It was in this laboratory and in my first-hand observation of President Horner's leadership where my own ideas and theories about institutional resiliency first took root.

Finally, this study and book could not have been completed without the unwavering encouragement and support of my husband, Glenn. Over the past several months, he has consistently and graciously indulged my need for time and space and has been my primary source of motivation since the study's inception.

In the end, this book belongs to those who shared so freely with me about their experiences and their institutions, and who obviously care very deeply about the future of their colleges and universities. I simply reported what I learned from them and I have tried to give this collective wisdom organization and meaning. My hope is that this book will be a helpful and encouraging resource to all who care about Christian higher education and who are working hard to ensure a strong future for their institutions.

Melissa Morriss-Olson
Vice President, Enrollment Management and Constituency Relations
North Park College, Chicago

CHAPTER ONE

Introduction and Overview of the Study

Introduction and Overview of the Study

"A specter is haunting higher education: the specter of decline and bankruptcy" (Keller, 1983).

The financial pressures facing most of American higher education have been well documented in recent years. In spite of substantial tuition and fee hikes and surprising enrollment growth (not withstanding earlier demographic projections to the contrary), coping with financial stress seems to have become the major challenge for many colleges and universities in the 1990s. While financial stress appears to be creating serious ripples throughout nearly all of higher education in the early 1990s (see *Campus Trends* Survey, 1995), the challenge is perhaps particularly troublesome for the small, special purpose institution, such as the Christian liberal arts college or university. With its limited resource base, its heavy reliance on tuition and fees, and its narrow mission and subsequent smaller base from which to draw students, the Christian liberal arts college or university faces unique constraints as it attempts to adapt to the changes taking place in all of higher education.

An overview of demographic and enrollment trends helps explain in part the challenges facing American higher education in general and the small, Christian college or university in particular.

Demographic and Enrollment Trends

One of the most significant issues facing higher education in recent years has been the projected, continual decline in high school graduates. The number of public high school graduates decreased from 3.2 million in 1976-77 to 2.4 million in 1985-86 (a decrease of 18%), rose to 2.5 million in 1987-88, and then decreased to 2.2 million in 1991-92. Overall, the size of the nation's public high school graduating class declined on average a total of 20 percent between 1979 and 1992. As Figure 1 shows, over the next several years, the number of high school graduates is expected to first fluctuate slightly and then begin a slow climb to a high of 3.3 million by the year 2007 (U.S. Department of Education, 1993). Moreover, educational demographic research agencies such as the Western Interstate Commission of Higher Education predict wide regional variation for higher education enrollments over the next decade. For example, while the Western state region enrollment is predicted to increase at the fastest rate between 1992 and 2009 (65% increase), enrollment in other regions is predicted to increase at a slower rate (an increase of 29% is predicted for the South/South-central region, 25% for the

Northeastern region, and 15% for the North-central region). Regarding the number of high school graduates (see Figure 2), the Western region (currently with the least number of high school graduates) is expected to overtake the Northeast region by the year 1997, and the North-central region by the year 2005 (Western Interstate Commission for Higher Education, 1992).

Figure 1. **Public and Nonpublic High School Graduates**
1978 to 2008 (projected)

- 2,806,950 in 1978
- 2,390,259 in 1985
- 2,618,160 in 1995
- 3,323,300 Projected in 2007

Source: Western Interstate Commission for Higher Education (1992).

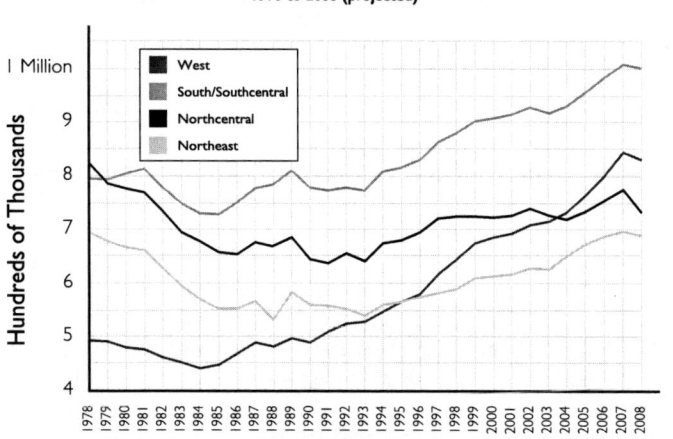

Figure 2. **Public and Nonpublic High School Graduates by Region**
1978 to 2008 (projected)

- West
- South/Southcentral
- Northcentral
- Northeast

Source: Western Interstate Commission for Higher Education (1992).

Survival Strategies for Christian Colleges and Universities

Interestingly, while the number of high school graduates decreased during the early 1980s, the projected decline in college enrollments failed to materialize in much of American higher education until only recently. To the surprise of many, colleges and universities experienced a 17 percent enrollment increase in the 1980s, from 12.1 million in 1980 to a record 14.4 million in 1993 (*The Chronicle of Higher Education: Almanac, 1993*). Enrollment in the private, 4-year sector increased from 2.4 million to 2.8 million during the same period (National Center for Educational Statistics, 1993). Analysts have offered a variety of explanations to account for this unexpected enrollment growth. For example, Hughes, Frances, and Lombardo (1991) suggest that increases in the college-going rate of both the traditional college-age and older population groups as well as increases in the number of women, minority, part-time, and foreign students during the past decade have been substantial enough to more than offset the projected enrollment decline. In the 1980s, for instance, enrollment among those in the 25-34 age group increased by 5 percent (from 3.1 million to 3.3 million), while enrollment in the 35+ age group increased by 46 percent (from 1.4 million to 2.1 million). According to Hughes, Frances, and Lombardo (1991), students in this latter category account for 86 percent of the unexpected enrollment increase of the 1980s. Other reasons given for the enrollment scenario of the 1980s include the greater intensity and sophistication applied by many colleges in the areas of recruitment and marketing, the development of institutional retention programs, and the employment of multiple revenue-generating strategies (Hamlin & Hungerford, 1988; Hossler, 1990; O'Keefe, 1989). Taken together, these factors seem to have compensated for the decline in traditional aged students.

Increased enrollments in colleges and universities have not necessarily resulted in improved financial conditions. During the last three decades, for example, academe lost a total of 337 institutions, the majority of which were private (see Table 1). The experience of the private sector as shown in Table 1 supports a belief held by some analysts: the "tough times" predicted to hit higher education since the mid 1970s, while delayed temporarily due to factors such as those described above, will take hold with great force in the early 1990s (Frances, 1986; Hauptman, 1990; Hughes, Frances, & Lombardo, 1991). Further support for this perspective is provided by recent *Campus Trends* survey results. In the most recent editions of this survey, which is administered to higher education administrators across the nation, financial issues were reported to be of paramount concern. For much of the public sector, basic funding has been cut back abruptly, despite continuing enrollment increases (nearly half reported stagnant or decreased operating budgets), and administrators are scrambling to deal with the consequences of this financial squeeze. Increased tuition and fees, increased class size and fewer class sections, faculty hiring freezes, new program postponement or cancellation, and reduced spending on building, equipment, and library acquisition are but a few of the effects noted by public university administrators (The American Council on Education, 1995).

Table 1. Institutions of Higher Education That Have Closed Their Doors 1960-61 to 1991-92

Year	All	Public 4-Year	Public 2-Year	Private 4-Year	Private 2-Year
1960 to 1964	25	0	6	4	15
1965 to 1969	70	0	10	29	30
1970 to 1974	98	0	17	48	33
1975 to 1979	43	1	1	28	13
1980 to 1984	26	0	0	21	5
1985 to 1991	75	0	2	37	36
Total	337	1	36	167	132

Source: U.S. Department of Education, Digest of Educational Statistics, (Washington, D.C.: National Center for Educational Statistics, 1992).

In the private sector, colleges face different but equally severe challenges. Many of these schools are confronting a decade-long financial squeeze, in which administrators have tried to keep their colleges affordable to a wide range of students while upgrading and improving the campus as resources are available. One third of the private colleges responding to the 1993 survey reported having made recent budget cuts with one-third expecting to make cuts in the near future. The most urgent financial stresses noted by the private college administrators include: funding needs for capital improvements and increasing financial aid costs, rising employee-related costs, enrollment uncertainty, and the challenge of cost containment in the face of increasing enrollment and increasing program needs (The American Council on Education, 1993). Taken together, the findings from both sectors highlight the fact that American higher education is clearly confronting difficult times.

Continuation of the increased enrollment patterns which in many cases have counterbalanced these financial pressures seems quite unlikely at this point. For instance, some are now beginning to predict the leveling off in the 1990s of the adult student market, a population upon which many institutions in the 1980s depended for balanced enrollments (Frances, 1986; Hauptman, 1990; Hughes, Frances, & Lombardo, 1991). And although 49% of colleges increased their first-time freshmen enrollment in 1993-94, this was down from 62% in 1988-89. Overall, nearly 36% of baccalaureate degree granting colleges reported decreases in entering freshman classes in 1993-94 with admissions directors at both public and private sector schools predicting smaller freshman classes for the next few years (*Campus Trends*, 1994).

Special Challenges Facing Christian Colleges and Universities

While challenges such as those described above are troublesome for all of higher education, the small, Christian liberal arts college or university appears to be particularly sensitive to turbulent times. For example, the sector fits well the description of the type of college predicted by many to be especially at risk to the challenges of the 1980s and 1990s. According to the conclusions of the 1980 National Institute of Independent Colleges and Universities study entitled *Private-College Openings, Closings, and Mergers, 1970-79*, the institutions most vulnerable to enrollment decline were typically "small, church-related, and coeducational" (p. 8). Such a scenario reflects the predictions of higher education authorities such as Fred E. Crossland, who hypothesized that the non-prestigious private colleges in a state with aggregate enrollment declines of 26% might expect to decline by nearly 50% in enrollment (Breneman, 1982, p. 28). Likewise, the 1980 Carnegie Council study entitled *Three Thousand Futures* identifies categories of vulnerability to enrollment decline, the most vulnerable being "the less selective liberal arts colleges and private two-year colleges" (p. 64).

A number of factors help explain why the Christian liberal arts college and university sector is so vulnerable to external forces. Perhaps most apparent is the fact that these institutions have carved out a more narrow mission focus, and thus have more limited resource pools from which to draw "funds and freshmen." For example, Christian liberal arts colleges and universities closely resemble the 494 colleges that Astin and Lee (1972) called "invisible" because of their smallness, limited resources, moderate selectivity, relative obscurity, and narrow mission. The lack of "visibility" coupled with the narrow mission focus introduces obvious constraints for these schools on several levels. For example, the range of students likely to be attracted to Christian liberal arts colleges and universities is

> *Christian liberal arts colleges and universities closely resemble the 494 colleges that Astin and Lee (1972) called "invisible" because of their smallness, limited resources, moderate selectivity, relative obscurity, and narrow mission.*

no doubt smaller than the pool of students available to admissions offices at less religious, four-year private institutions. As the competition for students across all of higher education has heated up in recent years, this factor becomes an especially important one.

A second factor involves fiscal resources. Historically, private higher education has relied quite heavily on tuition and fees and less on endowment and auxiliary enterprise income as major sources of institutional revenue. As noted by McPherson (1978), inordinate dependence on tuition revenue makes a college "more vulnerable to competitive factors that reduce demand, and also less able to innovate, experiment, and weather bad times" (p. 189). Recent data reveal a striking increase in recent years in the private sector's dependency on tuition and fee revenue, coupled with lesser increases in private gift and auxiliary enterprise income. For example, from Fiscal Year (FY) 1980-81 to Fiscal Year (FY) 1990-91, the percentage of general and educational revenue derived from tuition and fees for private institutions increased from 35.7% to 40.4%; this compares to an increase from 13.6% to 16.1% for public institutions during the same period (U.S. Department of Education, 1992). Inordinate tuition reliance may be an even greater problem for the Christian college and university sector. For example, tuition and fee revenue accounted in 1991 for an average of 54% of the total budget for the typical Christian college or university and as much as 89% of the budget at the smaller colleges in this sector (Morriss-Olson, 1995).

Increasing dependency on tuition and fee revenue is coupled with a second disturbing fiscal trend — a decline in private gift income. While a growing dependence on tuition revenue can be moderated somewhat by increasing revenue from other sources, it does not appear that this is the case for Christian colleges and universities. For example, research reveals an average 16% drop in private gift income at the Christian colleges and universities between 1981 and 1991. Likewise, in 1991, endowment income provided a mere 3% of the operational budget for these schools, compared to 6% for all private, four-year colleges (Morriss-Olson, 1995).

The Christian colleges and universities have been particularly hard-hit by the spiraling financial pressures mentioned earlier. Christian college and university administrators cite among their most pressing fiscal concerns the following: 1) the expense involved in increasing and maintaining faculty salaries at a level above the cost of living; 2) the cost of covering ever-increasing employee benefit expenses; 3) the cost of new buildings and plant maintenance, much of which was deferred during high inflationary periods; 4) the cost of keeping up with ever-burgeoning technology needs, as well as laboratory and other educational equipment; 5) the cost of administrative overhead; 6) the cost of augmenting dwindling federal and state student financial aid funds, and 7) the cost of strengthening recruitment and retention to offset competition by other institutions (Morriss-Olson, 1995). Taken together, such factors constitute an inordinate drain on any institution's budget but particularly, the small, Christian college or university's budget.

Some very clear patterns emerge when the implications of these various conditions are summarized. The small, less-selective, Christian college or university is potentially in a weak position in many of the areas discussed above. The demand for enrollment at these colleges already appears strained from price competition from the public sector. Highly dependent on tuition revenue yet lacking in substantial resources, such schools have been especially hard-hit by the spiraling costs which have impacted all of higher education in recent years. And, given its typically less-selective admissions stance, as well as its typically less-affluent student base, the small, Christian college is obviously vulnerable to further increases in the tuition gap between the public and private sectors; not to mention further changes in the structure of higher education which might make other sectors even more attractive to the very student it wishes to recruit.

The Warrant for the Report

A newly volatile and competitive era, brought on by profound demographic, social, economic, and political changes, has clearly confronted Christian college and university administrators with a battery of threats, challenges, and opportunities requiring thoughtful responses. Never before has the task of shaping the future of Christian colleges and universities demanded such concentration, imagination, and resourcefulness. Yet, despite these seemingly insurmountable challenges, there are many institutions of this type which appear to be weathering quite well the turbulence and pressures. O'Keefe (1989) reports on the extraordinary growth during the 1980s of a number of independent, four-year colleges, many of which had enrollments of less than 1,000 in the late 1970s. And, while a growing number of Christian colleges and universities are experiencing enrollment decline, a sizable number are reporting significant enrollment growth (Morriss-Olson, 1995). The obvious question raised then, is, given the adversity facing all small colleges, how might one account for those scattered instances of resiliency, particularly, those found among the less-visible, highly vulnerable, Christian liberal arts college and university sector?

The purpose of this report is to help the reader understand the factors which contribute to the resiliency of Christian liberal arts colleges and universities. The report uses as its basis the findings of a study which was conducted by the author in an attempt to: 1) gain an understanding of the current condition[1] of the Christian college and university sector, 2) gain an understanding of how the condition of the Christian college and university sector has changed over the past decade, 1981-1991, and 3) gain an understanding of why some Christian colleges and universities but not others have been able to achieve and/or maintain resiliency in the midst of a changing economic and political environment.

This report is significant in two important ways. First, virtually no research of this kind has been conducted using the Christian college and university sector as the sample population. Consequently, this report provides a contemporary portrayal of a sector which some researchers have described as "invisible" (Astin & Lee, 1972). As several researchers have noted, "invisible" institutions continue to be quite vulnerable to societal shifts and educational trends and frequently must undertake extensive institutional change in order to survive (Finkelstein, Farrar, & Pfinster, 1984; Zammuto, 1984). In light of this, the growth of the Christian college and university sector over the past decade is a phenomenon worth study. Second, very little research has been conducted within higher education which links the use of specific management strategies with operational outcomes. Consequently, this report provides valuable insight as to how strategy works generally, but particularly with regard to the Christian college or university setting. In brief, this report sheds light on two questions frequently asked by college or university administrators: "Are we doing the right things?" and "How do we know?" Such questions are especially pressing for Christian college and university leaders who must struggle to ensure that their institutions remain not only "visible" but also vibrant as they cultivate unique niches within the higher education arena. The breadth of this research further extends the work already conducted in the field and provides valuable and practical insights for Christian college and university administrators on "what works."

The obvious question raised then, is, given the adversity facing all small colleges, how might one account for those scattered instances of resiliency, particularly, those found among the less-visible, highly vulnerable, Christian liberal arts college and university sector?

---

[1] The term "condition" refers to the overall health and well-being of the institution and/or sector and is defined using a number of variables which have been identified in the research as having importance for the assessment of institutional performance. While the primary focus is on financial health, other variables have also been considered.

Survival Strategies for Christian Colleges and Universities

Study Methodology

The study was designed to answer four questions: 1) What is the current condition of the Christian liberal arts college and university sector and how has this condition changed during the decade of the 1980s? 2) What specific management strategies were used by the Christian liberal arts colleges and universities during the 1980s? 3) Is there a statistically significant relationship between what colleges did (i.e., what strategies they employed) and how they performed? 4) Do E.E. Chaffee's findings[2] regarding the usefulness of an "interpretive" strategy hold up for the Christian liberal arts college or university sector?

The population for the study includes the U.S. members of the Coalition for Christian Colleges & Universities, an association of "Christ-centered" institutions of the liberal arts and sciences (see Appendix A for a list of participating institutions). Participation in the study was limited to institutions for whom complete enrollment and financial data for each year of the ten-year period could be obtained. The final sample population consisted of 81 member institutions.[3]

Data were obtained for the study using the following methods: 1) enrollment data for each institution were gained from the 1981 to 1991 editions of the College Board Handbook, 2) financial data for each institution were obtained from the Quantum Research Corporation's CASPAR database, and 3) strategy usage data for each institution were acquired through the administration of the Strategic Management Survey, an instrument developed by the author and consisting of 220 management strategy items (see Appendix B for a copy of the survey). Strategies selected for inclusion in the survey were those fitting within Chaffee's strategic management typology for adaptive or interpretive strategy or those identified in the research as having importance for institutional performance. The survey was sent to the president of each participating insti-

---

[2]*Chaffee's research, which is reviewed in Chapter Three, involves the study of how a group of private colleges responded to severe financial stress during the 1970s. From her research, Chaffee developed a theory of strategic management to explain why some colleges, but not others, were able to rebound more quickly and more fully from declining conditions.*

[3]*Coalition institutions meet five criteria for membership: 1) a primary orientation as a four-year college or university with a curriculum rooted in the arts and sciences; 2) a public mission based upon the centrality of Jesus Christ and evidence of how faith is integrated with the institution's academic and student life programs; 3) a current hiring policy which requires of each full-time faculty member and administrator a personal faith in Jesus Christ; 4) a commitment to advancing the cause of Christian higher education through active participation in the Coalition, payment of annual fees, and institutional practices which are supportive of other Coalition members, and 5) institutional fund raising activities which are consistent with the standards of the Evangelical Council for Financial Accountability and demonstration of responsible financial operations.*

tution. Sixty-five presidents (or their designates) completed the survey, for a final response rate of 80%.

For analysis purposes, each institution was assigned an index rating, a measure incorporating the institution's performance (and "net changes" in that performance) on six key ratios (see Appendix C for more detail regarding the computation of the ratios) for each year of the ten-year period 1981 to 1991: 1) ratio of total assets to total liabilities; 2) ratio of endowment income to total educational and general revenues; 3) ratio of tuition and fee income to total educational and general revenues; 4) ratio of unrestricted funds balances to total expenditures and mandatory transfers; 5) ratio of net revenues to total revenues, and 6) FTE enrollment change 1981 to 1991. These specific indicators were measures which were identified in the literature (see, for example, Dickmeyer & Hughes, 1982) as being most appropriate for the assessment of the financial health of small, private colleges.[4] According to several observers (Dickmeyer and Hughes, 1982; Minter, 1978; Minter and Bowen, 1977; Minter, 1978; Minter, Hughes, Robinson, Turk, Buchanan, & Prager, 1982; Minter, Prager, Hughes, Robinson, & Turk, 1982, & Prinvale, 1992), the definition of fiscal health is multi-dimensional and ultimately eludes precision. Prinvale (1992) goes a step further in commenting that, "the selection of measures used to assess fiscal condition for an institution or a group of institutions is, ultimately, a subjective judgment" (p. 57). Thus, the specific variables which were selected to assess the financial condition of the colleges and universities in this study are wide-ranging in nature and include ratios which serve as warning signs of potential problems or fiscal vulnerability: financial strength (ratio 1), financial independence (ratio 2), tuition dependence (ratio 3), liquidity (ratio 4), annual operating performance (ratio 5), and market share (ratio 6).

---

[4]This study draws in part from a now classic project conducted in the early 1980s by Dickmeyer and Hughes (1982) involving the development of a multi-dimensional financial self-assessment framework. Dickmeyer and Hughes' framework emerged in a field project involving eight liberal arts colleges. In brief, these colleges were used to identify a series of indicators which, when considered together, proved to be the most powerful measures for assessing the overall condition of these colleges. The statistics chosen for this framework were selected from a broad spectrum of the college's activities to give a picture of the college's financial well-being. From their study, these authors define as financially healthy those colleges which "have the financial flexibility to respond to changes in the political, social, and economic environment in which they operate" (p.20). The major premise of Dickmeyer and Hughes' framework is that a college's overall condition can be characterized meaningfully by measuring available resources, trends in these resources, and the institution's special needs for these resources. The focus is on financial resources largely because of the authors' belief (based on their experience with the test colleges) that internal and external decisions and events affect these resources first. Since the amount and condition of an institution's resources are determined by both internal and external factors, changes in these resources are symptoms of those factors that cause institutional decline or improvement. According to these authors, a sufficient financial resource base provides a college with the ability to withstand environmental changes, and the flexibility to make changes at opportune times in response to these environmental changes as well as the luxury to experiment with mission or program "without concern that increased costs will curtail the entire operation" (Dickmeyer & Hughes, 1982, p. 21).

This index was then used to categorize[5] the institutions into one of three groups for analysis: 1) <u>Improving</u>: colleges or universities demonstrating significant increasing enrollment and financial performance between 1981 and 1991, 2) <u>Stable</u>: colleges or universities demonstrating moderately growing or stabilizing enrollment and financial performance between 1981 and 1991, and 3) <u>Declining</u>: colleges or universities demonstrating decreasing enrollment and financial performance between 1981 and 1991. Of the 65 responding institutions, 22 were categorized as Declining, 19 were Stable, and 24 were Improving institutions.

To address the research questions, a number of analytic procedures were conducted on the data including descriptive statistics, ANOVAS, the Tukey-B test, Pearson correlation coefficients, multiple regressions analyses,[6] and a qualitative treatment of the survey's open-ended responses. To test Chaffee's theory, the 220 survey items were regrouped into 10 new variables (following Chaffee's adaptive and interpretive typology). These variables were then used as independent variables in a final regression analysis.

---

[5]*Other factors considered in categorizing institutions included the number of ratios for which improvement was noted, performance on the enrollment and fund balance ratios (two measures identified in the research as having particular importance to institutional viability at small colleges), and institutional size. In addition, a number of other ratios and measures were examined and described in order to obtain a more comprehensive reading on the current condition of the sector as a whole. These measures include: 1) ratio of private gifts, grants, and contracts to total educational and general expenditures and mandatory transfers; 2) ratio of instruction to total educational and general revenues; 3) ratio of scholarships and fellowships to total educational and general revenues, and 4) market demand measures such as enrollment composition, the ratio of new student applications to acceptances, and the ratio of new student matriculants to completed applications.*

[6]*To ensure that differences in enrollment or revenue change were actually due to the use of specific strategies (versus intervening influences or variables), the institutions were compared in 1991 using means and multiple regression analysis on several key characteristics including: 1) tuition pricing; 2) number of academic programs; 3) financial aid as a percentage of educational and general expenditures; 4) proportion of full-time to part-time students; 5) proportion of resident to non-resident students; 6) proportion of in-state to out-of-state students; 7) proportion of full-time to part-time faculty; 8) admissions selectivity, and 9) endowment as a percentage of educational and general expenditures. These characteristics were used in the regression equations as independent variables for statistical control.*

Remaining Chapters

In Chapter Two, enrollment and other demographic variables will be reviewed to give the reader an up-to-date picture of the current condition of the Christian college and university sector. Chapter Three examines the literature and research which has been conducted in recent years and which provides a framework by which one might understand the factors which both facilitate and impede institutional resiliency. In Chapter Four, the characteristics which differentiate the Improving colleges and universities from the other institutions in the study are described and discussed. The report concludes with Chapter Five which offers practical suggestions and recommendations for Christian college and university administrators.

CHAPTER TWO

The Current Condition of the Christian College and University Sector

The Current Condition of the Christian College and University Sector

"It was the best of times, it was the worst of times"
(Charles Dickens).

These words of Charles Dickens depict well the world in which American colleges and universities have been situated in recent years. Turbulence, competitiveness, unpredictability, lean resources, and fluctuating revenues are just a few of the many challenges which have confronted institutional leaders during the past decade. Such challenges are especially pressing for Christian colleges and universities, institutions predicted by many to be particularly vulnerable to stressful conditions. How have these schools fared during the turbulent 1980s? What is the current condition of the sector? This chapter provides answers to these questions. Specifically, a variety of demographic variables are examined in order to provide the reader with an overall profile of the sector's[1] current condition and to describe how the condition of the sector has changed since 1981.

As defined in Chapter One, the term "condition" is used to refer to an institution's overall health and well-being. Assessment of the condition of the sector is built upon the individual assessments of each of the Coalition institutions using the various enrollment and financial variables identified in Chapter One. In general, "financially healthy" institutions are those which, based on their cumulative performance on this set of variables, appear to have sufficient flexibility to respond to changes in the external environment in which they operate.

Burgeoning Undergraduate and FTE Enrollments

Clark's 1989 report on the status of the Coalition sector depicted a worsening enrollment scenario for a considerable number of these schools. Data obtained in the current study suggest that the impending enrollment crisis predicted by Clark has been averted. For example, since the mid 1980s, the Coalition institutions in the aggregate have been experiencing stronger enrollment growth than the national average for all private four-year colleges. The mean undergraduate headcount increased by 12% between 1981 and 1991, compared to 5% for all four-year privates (see Table 2). As shown in Table 3, FTE increased over the same decade at a rate on par with the

---

[1] As noted in Chapter One, the sector includes the U.S. members of the Coalition for Christian Colleges & Universities for whom complete enrollment and financial data could be obtained.

national average (12%). In general, the Coalition schools fared worse than average during the first half of the 1980s and much better than average during the latter half of the decade. Most significantly, more of the Coalition schools are experiencing a growing FTE with the average increase much greater than was reported by Clark in his 1989 study. As of 1991, 54 of the 81 schools increased FTE during the 1980s, with an average increase of 41%. An average decrease of 16% was reported by the 27 schools experiencing a declining FTE. Clark's study which spanned the early 1980s, i.e. 1980 - 1986, found only 30 schools experiencing FTE gains with an average increase of 14%. Of the 41 schools in Clark's study experiencing a declining FTE, the average decrease was 12%.

For many of the Coalition colleges, it appears that enrollment gains have come from increasing part-time and transfer student enrollments. Part-time undergraduate headcount enrollments increased by 53% during the 1980s, compared to a mere 8% increase for full-time undergraduate headcount. The increasing part-time enrollment trend is a disturbing one,

Table 2. **Undergraduate Enrollment Change by Headcount by Group 1981 to 1991**

	CCCU Schools				
	All 81 91	Improving 81 91	Stable 81 91	Declining 81 91	All 4-year Privates 81 91
Averages:					
Total	1013 1139	872 1213	1165 1219	1040 993	1629 171
% Change 81-91	12%	39%	5%	-5%	5%
Full-time	918 996	792 1047	1043 1059	951 889	1438 149
% Change 81-91	8%	32%	2%	-7%	4%
Part-time	98 150	84 171	122 168	92 112	326 345
% Change 81-91	53%	103%	38%	22%	6%

Source: U.S. Department of Education, Digest of Educational Statistics, (Washington, D.C.: National Center for Educational Statistics, 1993).

Table 3. **Enrollment Change by FTE by Group 1981 to 1991**

	CCCU Schools				
	All	Improving	Stable	Declining	All 4-year Privates
Year					
1981	993	866	1139	1009	n/a
1986	957	909	1101	888	n/a
1991	1115	1181	1217	962	n/a
% Change					
1981-1986	-4%	5%	3%	-14%	5%
1986-1991	16%	30%	1%	8%	6%
1981-1991	12%	36%	7%	-5%	12%

Source: U.S. Department of Education, Digest of Educational Statistics, (Washington, D.C.: National Center for Educational Statistics, 1993).

Survival Strategies for Christian Colleges and Universities

particularly when it accompanies a declining full-time enrollment. For example, the financial difficulties encountered by the Declining[2] colleges in the study were no doubt accelerated in part by a corresponding shift in the enrollment composition. As Table 2 shows, the full-time undergraduate headcount at the Declining colleges decreased an average of 7% between 1981 and 1991 (this was accompanied by a 22% increase in the part-time headcount). Since part-time students typically generate less revenue for the institution (for example, they take fewer credits frequently paying a discounted tuition rate, and they usually live at home), an enrollment shift such as that experienced by the Declining colleges can prove financially lethal over time. While the Improving colleges also experienced a significant part-time undergraduate enrollment increase (103%), these colleges also increased in full-time enrollment (32%). The increase in part-time enrollment was more modest among the Stable colleges (38%) as was the full-time enrollment increase (2%).

Undergraduate Student Demographic Trends

While the proportion of part-time to full-time undergraduate enrollment increased in the aggregate from 10% to 13% between 1981 and 1991, the Coalition schools continue to enroll a primarily full-time, residential undergraduate population. In 1991, approximately 87% of the Coalition undergraduate enrollment was full-time compared to a national average for all four-year private liberal arts colleges of 80%. Coalition schools on average have become more residential over the past decade (see Table 4). Approximately 80% of the student population resided on campus at Coalition schools in 1991 compared to 76% in 1981. Moreover, the sector is considerably more residential than the norm. For example, in 1991, the national on-campus residence average for four-year privates was 69%. Since their inception, the Coalition schools have claimed as a central distinctive an educational experience which impacts all aspects of the student's life. Such a distinctive would be nearly impossible to realize without a significant investment on the student's part in the life of the campus. On the surface, the high percentage of Coalition students living on campus and enrolled full-time suggests that these schools have generally not strayed very far from their original focus.

---

[2]As noted in Chapter One, the 65 participating institutions were placed into one of three groups for analysis: 1) Improving (colleges demonstrating significant increasing enrollment and financial performance between 1981 and 1991), 2) Stable (colleges demonstrating moderately growing or stabilizing enrollment and financial performance between 1981 and 1991), and 3) Declining (colleges demonstrating decreasing enrollment and financial performance between 1981 and 1991).

Table 4. **Change in Student Demographics by Group 1981 to 1991**

	CCCU Schools								All 4-year Privates	
	All		Improving		Stable		Declining			
	81	91	81	91	81	91	81	91	81	91
% Residing on Campus	76%	80%	73%	81%	80%	82%	77%	78%	n/a	69%
% Commuting	24%	20%	27%	19%	20%	18%	23%	22%	n/a	31%

Source: U.S. Department of Education, Digest of Educational Statistics, (Washington, D.C.: National Center for Educational Statistics, 1993).

On the down side, the Coalition schools have made only marginal gains in increasing the ethnic diversity of their student bodies between 1981 and 1991 (see Table 5). The percentage of the student body comprised of persons from minority backgrounds increased only slightly during this period, from an average of 7% in 1981 to 9% in 1991. At four-year privates nationally, ethnic minority student representation increased from 15% to 19% during this same period. Despite the significantly less diverse student population on Coalition campuses, only one survey respondent noted as a critical concern for the future the need to increase campus diversity. Whether the lack of diversity at Coalition schools is intentional, whether Coalition institution administrators have necessarily been drawn to other concerns and agendas, or whether minorities simply do not find the Christian college campus and culture a welcoming ethos is not clear. However, given the increasing globalization of American society and given the fact that much of the new growth in higher education in future years is predicted to come from ethnic minority groups, as well as imperatives derived from the Christian mission which undergirds Coalition institutions, the lack of progress on this front is disconcerting and deserves further attention.

Table 5. **Change in Student Demographics by Group 1981 to 1991**

	CCCU Schools								All 4-year Privates	
	All		Improving		Stable		Declining			
	81	91	81	91	81	91	81	91	81	91
% Minority Students	7%	9%	7%	9%	5%	8%	7%	9%	15%	19%
% Foreign Students	3%	3%	4%	3%	3%	3%	3%	4%	3%	4%

Source: U.S. Department of Education, Digest of Educational Statistics, (Washington, D.C.: National Center for Educational Statistics, 1993).

The Move into Graduate Education

Graduate enrollment increased at Coalition schools on average by 25% during the 1980s (see Table 6). And, as shown in Table 7, the number of schools offering at least one graduate program has jumped from 21 in 1981 to 40 in 1991.

Table 6. Graduate Enrollment Change by Headcount by Group 1981 to 1991

	All 81	All 91	Improving 81	Improving 91	Stable 81	Stable 91	Declining 81	Declining 91
Total	223	279	268	306	233	336	160	168
% Change 81-91		25%		14%		31%		5%
Full-time	102	99	129	112	71	97	121	82
% Change 81-91		-0.30%		-14%		37%		-32%
Part-time	147	200	139	224	202	244	86	110
% Change 81-91		36%		62%		21%		28%

Table 7. Change in Programmatic Variables by Group

	All 81	All 91	Improving 81	Improving 91	Stable 81	Stable 91	Declining 81	Declining 91
Number of Undergraduate Programs:								
Mean	27	32	23	31	29	35	30	32
Range - Min.	5	10	5	10	7	14	5	13
Max.	54	75	50	65	54	75	54	57
Number of Graduate Programs:								
Mean	5	4	6	5	6	4	3	3
Range - Min.	0	0	0	0	0	0	0	0
Max.	13	27	9	27	16	11	13	16
Number of Schools Offering Grad Programs:								
0 Programs	44	25	18	10	9	4	17	11
1 - 4 Programs	12	32	2	13	4	7	6	12
5 - 9 Programs	7	3	5	1	2	2	0	0
10+ Programs	2	5	0	2	1	2	1	1
Number of Full-time Faculty:								
Mean	57	68	50	63	63	75	60	66
Mean Student/ Faculty Ratio	16/1	15/1	16/1	16/1	17/1	14/1	16/1	14/1

Survival Strategies for Christian Colleges and Universities

Nevertheless, the majority of the schools offer only a handful of programs at the graduate level; of the 39 schools offering graduate programs in 1991, 32 (82%) offer 4 or fewer programs suggesting that the Coalition schools remain primarily focused on the undergraduate experience. Moreover, the Coalition schools continue to offer a fairly narrow range of undergraduate programs (an average of 32 in 1991 versus 27 in 1981), suggesting that students are attracted to these colleges for reasons other than program breadth and variety in program offerings. This contradicts the findings cited by several studies (Breneman, 1982; Buffington, 1990; Cohen, 1983; St. John, 1991; Zammuto, 1983) in which academic program breadth and number of programs offered were found to correlate positively with enrollment growth. The faculty-to-student ratio on average has changed little over the past decade (15:1 in 1991 versus 16:1 in 1981), meaning that students enrolled in Coalition schools most likely continue to receive the kind of personal attention and support from faculty that these colleges are noted for providing.

Enrollment Changes by Region and Location

There are vast differences in how the Coalition schools have fared enrollment-wise by region as well as by location. For example, institutions located in the South/South-central and Northeastern regions of the country fared much better than expected during the 1980s, posting respective undergraduate enrollment increases of 29% and 20% (see Table 8). Institutions located in the Western and Northcentral regions of the country fared less well, recording enrollment increases of 11% and 2%, respectively. Taking into account regional differences in the declining high school graduation pool as well as national college growth rates for all four-year private colleges between 1981 and 1991, the Coalition schools in the Northeastern and South/South-central did better than might have been expected, schools in the Western region performed about on par with the national norms, and schools in the Northcentral region of the country performed much worse than expected.

With regard to location, Coalition schools in rural and suburban areas experienced stronger enrollment growth on average during the 1980s than schools located in urban areas. As shown in Table 9, more than half of the Declining colleges are located either in very large cities or in large towns (59% versus 39% for Improving colleges), while more than half of the Improving colleges are located in rural communities, small towns, and small cities (61% versus 41% for Declining colleges). This finding contradicts an earlier study (Tempel, 1985) wherein

Table 8. **Location of Schools by Region by Group**

Region	All Colleges	Improving	Stable	Declining
Northeast	9 (11%)	4	2	3
Western	19 (23%)	7	6	6
South/S.C.	23 (28%)	10	7	6
Northcentral	30 (37%)	7	9	14

		Change in FTE Enrollment 1981 - 1991	
Region	% Decline in HS Grads 1981 - 1991	CCCU Schools	All 4 - Yr Privates
Western	-2%	11%	15%
South/S.C.	-11%	29%	12%
Northcentral	-25%	2%	12%
Northeast	-29%	20%	-6%

Note: States included in each region are as follows:
Northeast: NH, VT, ME, NY, PA, MD, DC, DE, NJ, CT, RI, MASS
South/S.C.: TX, LA, MISS, AL, GA, FL, OK, AR, TN, KT, WV, VA, NC, SC
Northcentral: ND, SD, NE, KS, MN, IA, MO, WI, IL, MI, IN, OH
Western: WA, OR, CA, NE, AZ, NM, CO, UT, WY, MT, ID, AL, HI

Source: U.S. Department of Education, Digest of Educational Statistics, (Washington, D.C.: National Center for Educational Statistics, 1993).

Table 9. **Location of Coalition Schools by Environment and Location by Group**

	All Colleges	Improving	Stable	Declining
Environment:				
Urban	11	5	2	4
Suburban	45	14	14	17
Rural	25	9	8	8
Location:				
Very Large City	14	5	3	6
Large Town	24	6	8	11
Small City	18	8	6	4
Small Town	14	3	4	7
Rural Community	11	6	3	1

Source: U.S. Department of Education, Digest of Educational Statistics, (Washington, D.C.: National Center for Educational Statistics, 1993).

urban colleges were found to be in better enrollment and financial health than rural institutions. Such findings suggest that the urban setting may be potentially disadvantageous for a Christian college or university. The type of student (and parent) typically drawn to a Christian college experience may be more attracted to a campus that is at least minimally set apart somewhat from the rest of the world. In any event, these findings suggest that location and changes in the drawing pool of eligible high school students had differing effects on the enrollment performance of the Coalition schools and may have impacted to varying degrees the well being of particular schools during the 1980s.

Enrollment Changes by Institutional Size

The findings of this study contradict in one other important way the Tempel study mentioned above. Specifically, Tempel found that larger institutions (students enrolling 2,000 or more students) were better equipped to deal with decline. This finding does not appear to hold up for the schools in this study. For example, Table 10 shows that 71% of the Improving colleges had enrollments of less than 1,000 in 1981. (Some analysts have suggested that an institutional size of 1,000 is a minimum threshold for institutional viability.) Moreover, in 1981, the bulk of the smaller-sized schools consisted primarily of Improving and Declining colleges. However, in 1991, the percentage of smaller-sized Improving and Stable colleges had dropped from 71% to 55% and from 46% to 42%, respectively, while the percentage of smaller-sized Declining colleges increased slightly (from 62% to 69%). Clearly, institutional size does not appear to play a major role in explaining a growing or declining condition. Furthermore, small size does not seem to inhibit an institution's efforts towards growth and resiliency.

Coalition schools in rural and suburban areas experienced stronger enrollment growth on average during the 1980s than schools located in urban areas.

Table 10. Enrollment Change by Institutional Size by Group 1981 to 1991

	All 81	All 91	Improving 81	Improving 91	Stable 81	Stable 91	Declining 81	Declining 91
FTE:								
Fewer than 499	17	12	9	4	1	1	7	7
500 - 999	32	34	11	12	10	9	11	13
1,000 - 1,499	19	23	4	8	7	9	8	6
1,500 - 1,999	7	6	4	4	3	1	0	1
2,000 and above	6	6	0	0	3	4	3	2
Total	81	81	28	28	24	24	29	29
% of Schools with Enrollment:								
999 or less	60%	57%	71%	55%	46%	42%	62%	69%
1,000 or above	40%	43%	29%	45%	54%	58%	38%	31%

Freshman Headcount and Admissions Trends

Given the sector's historical dependence on the traditional 18-22 year-old recruitment pool, it is also instructive to examine trends and changes in the first-year student population. As shown in Table 11, freshman enrollment trends between 1981 and 1991 fared slightly less well than total undergraduate FTE and headcount patterns. Freshman enrollments declined in the

Survival Strategies for Christian Colleges and Universities

aggregate 9% during this period with the decrease taking place in the first half of the 1980s. Since 1986, schools in all three groups have fared much better with the Improving colleges showing the most significant increase in freshman enrollment. However, compared to national norms, the Coalition schools have declined in the aggregate in freshman enrollments at a slightly higher pace (-9% versus -6%). Improving colleges fared much better than national averages while both Stable and Declining colleges fared worse than average. These data provide further support for the notion that for those schools experiencing enrollment growth during the 1980s, the increase has come less from traditional sources (i.e., first-time, 18 year old college students) than from new or alternative markets (i.e., adult, part-time, graduate). In fact, for Stable and Declining colleges, the enrollment shortfall during the 1980s appears to be attributable in large part to a declining traditional freshman population.

Table 11. **Freshman Headcount Change by Group 1981 to 1991**

	CCCU Schools				All 4-year Privates
	All	Improving	Stable	Declining	
Average Headcount In Year:					
1981	298	253	349	305	399
1986	249	239	275	236	n/a
1991	273	308	271	237	376
% Headcount Change:					
1981 to 1986	-20%	-6%	-21%	-29%	n/a
1986 to 1991	10%	29%	-2%	0%	n/a
1981 to 1991	-9%	22%	-29%	-29%	-6%

Source: U.S. Department of Education, Digest of Educational Statistics, (Washington, D.C.: National Center for Educational Statistics, 1993).

Table 12 shows the aggregate change rates from 1981 to 1991 in new student conversion ratios as well as rates for the three comparison groups. While yield rates have slipped nationally and among the Coalition schools, some interesting differences between the national averages and the Coalition sector can be noted. First, while the national acceptance rate for four-year private colleges increased slightly between 1981 and 1991, the rate decreased slightly for Coalition schools. In particular, acceptance rates decreased among Improving and Declining colleges, suggesting a possible tightening of admissions standards among schools in these two groups. Since freshman enrollments are also on the rise at these schools, one might speculate about the possible relationship between enhanced academic quality and increased enrollment.

Nevertheless, compared to national norms, Coalition schools are on average still accepting a much higher percentage of applicants (81% versus 63%), a factor which greatly increases this sector's vulnerability to enrollment fluctuations.

Table 12. **Change in Freshman Enrollment Yields by Group 1981 to 1991**

Enrollment Yields by Group	% Apps Accepted 81	% Apps Accepted 91	% Apps Enrolled 81	% Apps Enrolled 91	% Accepts Enrolled 81	% Accepts Enrolled 91
All CCCU Schools	87%	81%	61%	49%	71%	61%
% Change 1981 to 1991		-6%		-13%		-10%
Improving	89%	80%	61%	51%	68%	64%
% Change 1981 to 1991		-8%		-10%		-4%
Stable	86%	86%	65%	49%	76%	57%
% Change 1981 to 1991		0%		16%		-19%
Declining	86%	78%	60%	46%	70%	60%
% Change 1981 to 1991		-8%		14%		-10%
All 4-Year Privates	60%	63%	n/a	n/a	50%	39%
% Change 1981 to 1991		-3%		n/a		-10%

Source: U.S. Department of Education, Digest of Educational Statistics, (Washington, D.C.: National Center for Educational Statistics, 1993).

For Stable and Declining colleges, the enrollment shortfall during the 1980s appears to be attributable in large part to a declining traditional freshman population.

The accepted applicant yield rate declined in the aggregate for Coalition schools at about the same pace as for all four-year private colleges (-10%). Again, it is interesting to note the differences between the three Coalition groups (see Table 12). While the Stable colleges experienced the sharpest drop in the conversion of applicants and accepted students, Improving colleges fared much better than average. A higher applicant acceptance rate (as is the case for the Stable colleges) could mean a less qualified prospect pool, thus accounting for a steeper drop-off as one moves down the enrollment funnel. In any event, the Improving colleges are clearly outperforming national norms with regard to freshman enrollment trends. The picture is considerably more mixed for the Stable and Declining college groups.

Several additional admissions characteristics were examined in this study with the results displayed in Table 13. For example, of the 65 responding institutions, 3 classify themselves as having an open-door admissions policy, 57 have selective, and 5 have competitive admissions standards. In the Improving and Declining groups, all but one in each group classify themselves as selective. The Stable colleges are also primarily selective; however, four colleges in this group are competitive and two have open-door policies.[3]

Table 13. **Admissions Characteristics by Group**

	All	Improving	Stable	Declining
Self-Reported Selectivity in 1991:				
Open-Door	3	0	2	1
Selective	57	23	13	21
Competitive	5	1	4	0
+Self-Reported Change in Admissions Standards 1981 to 1991:				
General Selectivity	3.86	4.17	3.72	3.63
Level/Years High School Work	3.48	3.62	3.55	3.27
High School GPA/Rank	3.79	4.00	3.67	3.68
ACT/SAT Schores	3.81	4.00	3.83	3.59

+Rating Scale: 1=Much Lower   3=No Change   5=Much Higher

	All 81	All 91	Improving 81	Improving 91	Stable 81	Stable 91	Declining 81	Declining 91
Enrollment Strategy Pursued in 1980s and 1990s:								
Increase Enrollments	53	58	20	20	16	17	17	21
Maintain/Stabilize Enrollments	10	6	3	3	3	2	4	1
Reduce Enrollments	1	0	0	0	0	0	1	0

Not surprisingly, there seems to be greater concern among the Coalition schools for increasing enrollment in the 1990s than was the case a decade ago (see Table 13). While no school intends to reduce enrollments in the 1990s (this compares to one in the 1980s), and while a handful intend to maintain enrollments (12 in the 1990s versus 20 in the 1980s), the majority of schools (72%) report an intent to increase enrollments during the next several years. The shift is most significant among Declining colleges where the number of colleges planning enrollment increases has jumped from 17 to 21.

With regard to self-reported admissions standards, while no college reported a lowering of standards during the 1980s on any of the items listed in Table 13, the Improving colleges

---

[3]*Definitions of the selective, competitive, and open-door admissions standards are as follows: Open-door - admit all who wish to attend, or admit any high school graduate. Selective - admit the majority of applicants who meet some specified level of achievement or other qualifications above and beyond high school graduation. Competitive - admit only a limited number of those applicants who meet specified levels of academic achievement or other qualifications above and beyond high school graduation.*

From: AACRAO. (1986). <u>Demographics, Standards and Equity: Challenges in College Admissions.</u> New York: College Board Publications, p. 7.

reported a significant strengthening of standards compared to Declining and Stable colleges. This appears to support the notion that Improving and Declining colleges are perhaps raising their admissions standards. However, it does not explain the apparent contradiction between self-reported higher standards and a flat admissions acceptance rate at Stable colleges. It could be that Stable colleges perceive their standards to be higher than what is actually the case, or that the pool from which all three groups draw has changed significantly over the past decade.

Table 14. **Change in Student Demographics by Group 1981 to 1991**

	All 81	91	Improving 81	91	Stable 81	91	Declining 81	91
% Freshman Admitted Provisionally	2%	8%	2%	9%	2%	8%	1%	8%
% Freshman Taking Remedial Coursework	2%	11%	2%	12%	2%	13%	2%	10%

At the same time, schools across the Coalition sector report an aggregate increase of about 11% in the percentage of provisionally admitted freshmen and freshmen needing remediation in basic skill areas (see Table 14). Whether Coalition schools are actually enrolling less well-prepared students or whether they are simply giving more attention to these students (e.g., a retention strategy receiving increasing attention on many campuses involves identifying and assisting underprepared students) than they did ten years ago is unclear. Because there are no national norms for this variable, it is difficult to assess change in this area vis-à-vis other institutions.

A particularly interesting finding and one contradictory to previous research involves the breadth of an institution's student recruitment pool. Previously conducted research (Hilpert, 1987; Zammuto, 1983) suggested that colleges with primarily national markets sustained enrollments significantly better than colleges which draw their students primarily from within the state. The reason offered by researchers was that because changes in the size of the high school pool and economic conditions varied substantially from state-to-state, colleges with broader drawing markets were better equipped to weather turbulent times. This study found that colleges improving in enrollment during the 1980s drew a higher percentage of students from within state than colleges with decreasing enrollments (see Table 15). Since this finding mirrors what Buffington found in her 1990 study, and since the population for both studies included less-selective, private liberal arts colleges, one could speculate that this finding may be unique to small, less well-established private colleges. For example, as families became increasingly concerned during the latter half of the 1980s about spiraling college costs, they may have been more willing to pay the price to send a child across the country to a prestigious private college than to a small, less-distinguished Christian college. Subsequently, less prestigious Christian colleges dependent upon a national pool of students may have been disadvantaged as growing numbers of students began choosing colleges closer to home or colleges with stronger reputations. At the same time, Christian colleges with strong regional reputations and large in-state recruitment pools may have had an advantage in the face of these changing dynamics.

Table 15. **Change in Student Demographics by Group 1981 to 1991**

	\multicolumn{8}{c}{CCCU Schools}								All 4-year Privates	
	All		Improving		Stable		Declining		All 4-year Privates	
	81	91	81	91	81	91	81	91	81	91
% In-State Students	56%	56%	64%	63%	54%	55%	49%	50%	57%	57%
% Out-of-State Students	44%	44%	36%	37%	46%	45%	51%	50%	43%	43%

Source: U.S. Department of Education, <u>Digest of Educational Statistics</u>, (Washington, D.C.: National Center for Educational Statistics, 1993).

Trends in Financial Measures

Particularly for the Declining colleges, a decreasing faculty-to-student ratio, coupled with declining enrollment and increasing fixed cost expenses, sets the stage for impending fiscal distress. Without new or increasing revenue streams to offset this downward spiraling financial picture, these schools indeed face significant challenges. Several variables describing the financial condition of the institution in greater detail were examined and are reported in Table 16 through Table 22. Taken together, these variables provide a mixed picture regarding the overall health of this sector.

One of the most common means of communicating an institution's financial condition is the balance sheet, a report showing the financial position of the institution at a given point in time, such as the end of the fiscal year. The balance sheet ratio used in this study is the ratio of unrestricted fund balances to total expenditures and mandatory transfers. In brief, this ratio describes the institution's ability to support its current level of operations from all available expendable resources without considering revenues generated from operations. As such, this ratio is an important measure of financial strength relative to institutional operating size.

Table 16. Change in Financial Ratio: Unrestricted Funds Balance to Total Expenditures and Mandatory Transfers by Group 1981 to 1991

	\multicolumn{8}{c}{CCCU Schools}
	\multicolumn{2}{c}{All}	\multicolumn{2}{c}{Improving}	\multicolumn{2}{c}{Stable}	\multicolumn{2}{c}{Declining}
Ratios	81	91	81	91	81	91	81	91
Mean Ratio	0.04	0.03	-0.06	0.08	0.08	0.07	0.11	-0.07
Range - Min.	-0.70	-1.49	-0.70	-0.10	-0.14	0.00	-0.14	-1.49
Max.	0.49	0.26	0.27	0.26	0.26	0.23	0.49	0.25
Mean % Change	\multicolumn{2}{c}{6%}	\multicolumn{2}{c}{378%}	\multicolumn{2}{c}{129%}	\multicolumn{2}{c}{-450%}
Number of Schools With Ratios:								
(.500) and below	1	2	1	0	0	0	0	2
(.001)-(.499)	24	14	16	3	3	1	5	10
.001-.099	30	41	9	16	11	15	10	10
.100-.199	17	17	3	8	6	5	8	4
.200-.299	7	7	0	2	4	3	3	2
.300-.399	2	0	0	0	1	0	1	0
.400-.499	0	0	0	0	0	0	1	0
.500 and up	0	0	0	0	0	0	0	0

Source: National Science Foundation CASPAR Database System.

While no absolute value for fiscal health has been identified for this ratio, Rothschild, Unterberg, Towbin, and Peat, Marwick, Mitchell and Company (1984) suggest that a ratio of 0.3:1 or better is needed to reinforce significantly the ratio of expendable fund balances to plant debt. According to these financial analysts, a ratio of 0.3:1 or better suggests that an institution is able to support its current level of operations from all available expendable resources without diverting revenues generated from operations, thus providing the institution with a reasonable margin of protection against the possibility of adversity. As shown in Table 16, the aggregate mean ratio for all Coalition schools falls well below this minimum threshold (indeed, the mean ratio declined from .039:1 in 1981 to .026:1 in 1991). In fact, no school had a ratio above the suggested threshold of 0.3:1 in 1991. Improving colleges have clearly fared better than Declining colleges on this ratio, with Stable colleges experiencing only slight change. For example, while a large portion of the Improving colleges had negative fund balance ratios in 1981 (17 out of 28), only three such schools had negative ratios in 1991. Inversely, while only a handful of the Declining schools had negative ratios in 1981 (5 out of 29), the situation is much worse in 1991 (12 out

Fewer schools are living within their means in 1991 than was the case ten years ago and, even for those schools experiencing enrollment and tuition revenue increases, expenses appear to be increasing at a rate greater than what revenue income will support.

of 29). Overall, the Coalition schools experienced an average mean increase of 6% on this ratio between 1981 and 1991 with Improving and Stable colleges showing the most significant gains (+378% and +129% respectively). On the other hand, the Declining colleges lost significant ground (-450%).

After assessing overall financial condition, financial analysts typically focus in on the primary causes that produced the financial condition described by the balance sheet ratios. To better comprehend financial performance, such analysts typically turn to the financial activities reported for current funds, or what are commonly called net operating ratios. The net operating ratio used in this study is the ratio of net total revenues to total revenues, an indicator used to measure whether total current operations for any given year resulted in a surplus or deficit. The ratio is calculated by dividing the annual total revenues amount (i.e., all current unrestricted and restricted funds revenues) into the annual net revenues amount (i.e., all current unrestricted and restricted funds revenues less all current funds expenditures and mandatory transfers). A positive ratio indicates a surplus for the year reported on. In general, the larger the surplus, the stronger the institution's financial position as a result of the year's operation. Large deficits in several successive years indicate the strong possibility of a seriously weakening financial condition. Since a large surplus or deficit directly affects the size of unrestricted fund balances, this ratio is one of the primary indicators of the underlying causes of the institution's financial condition.

As is evident by the data presented in Table 17, the mean ratio for all schools steadily declined between 1981 and 1991 with the Declining colleges experiencing the most significant decrease and the Stable colleges experiencing the least. It appears that since 1989 schools in all three groups experienced slippage on this ratio with all groups showing negative mean ratios in 1991. This suggests that fewer schools are living within their means in 1991 than was the case ten years ago and, even for those schools experiencing enrollment and tuition revenue increases, expenses appear to be increasing at a rate greater than what revenue income will support.

Further analysis of revenues by source and expenditures by function provides additional insight on the findings reported above. For example, the data in Table 18 show that the Coalition schools are drawing a greater share of their revenue from tuition and fee income than was the case in the early 1980s (47% in 1981 versus 54% in 1991). While this increase appears to be on par with national norms, the Coalition schools are considerably more dependent on tuition income than other

Table 17. Change in Financial Ratio: Net Revenues to
Total Revenues by Group 1981 to 1991

CCCU Schools

Mean Ratio by Group

Year:	All	Improving	Stable	Declining
1981	.0156	-.0137	.0365	.0306
1982	.0121	.0039	.0312	.0059
1983	.0075	.0211	.0135	-.0127
1984	.0038	.0159	.0133	-.0181
1985	-.0022	.0022	.0096	-.0159
1986	.0123	.0408	.0105	-.0181
1987	-.0046	.0249	-.0233	-.0215
1988	-.0199	.0155	-.0247	-.0677
1989	-.0287	-.0375	-.0193	-.0263
1990	-.0148	.0088	-.0221	-.0345
1991	-.0216	-.0207	-.0041	-.0363
Mean % Change	224%	-121%	-70.30%	-460%

Source: National Science Foundation CASPAR Database System.

four-year privates colleges. Moreover, the combination of higher applicant acceptance rates and increasing tuition dependency puts these schools in a much more vulnerable position vis-à-vis enrollment fluctuation. Given the relatively small to non-existent cushion that many of these schools are living with (i.e., fund balance ratios), there appears to be very little flexibility for responding to severe crisis should the need arise.

Likewise, income from private gifts and grants at Coalition schools is clearly not keeping pace with expenses. The decline appears to be most pronounced for Improving and Declining colleges. As shown in Table 19, the percentage of the education budget met by private gifts and grants income declined from 17% in 1981 to 12% in 1991. While the mean percentage for

Table 18. Change in Financial Ratio:
Tuition and Fee Revenues to Total E & G Revenues
by Group 1981 to 1991

CCCU Schools

	All 81	All 91	Improving 81	Improving 91	Stable 81	Stable 91	Declining 81	Declining 91	All 4-year Privates 81	All 4-year Privates 91
Mean Ratio	0.47	0.54	0.48	0.55	0.47	0.53	0.46	0.53	0.37	0.41
Range - Min.	0.23	0.34	0.23	0.38	0.31	0.34	0.36	0.40	n/a	n/a
Max.	0.89	0.78	0.89	0.78	0.59	0.69	0.61	0.65	n/a	n/a
Mean % Change	15%		19%		13%		15%		32%	

Source: National Science Foundation CASPAR Database System.

Survival Strategies for Christian Colleges and Universities

1991 is still slightly above the national average for similar schools, the magnitude of the decline for Coalition schools over the past decade is much more significant. Such a decline suggests that private giving is declining, that educational and general expenditures are rising faster than this source of funding, or both. Such a decline must be offset by increasing revenues elsewhere (most likely tuition and fees or endowment) or by reducing expenditures.

Table 19. **Change in Financial Ratio: Private Gifts and Grants to Total Expenditures and Mandatory Transfers by Group 1981 to 1991**

	\multicolumn{8}{c}{CCCU Schools}	All 4-year Privates	
	All 81	All 91	Improving 81	Improving 91	Stable 81	Stable 91	Declining 81	Declining 91	81	91
Mean Ratio	0.17	0.12	0.18	0.12	0.15	0.11	0.18	0.13	0.11	0.09
Range - Min.	0.04	0.03	0.04	0.03	0.04	0.05	0.08	0.06	n/a	n/a
Max.	0.55	0.27	0.55	0.27	0.32	0.24	0.39	0.23	n/a	n/a
Mean % Change 1981 - 1991	\multicolumn{2}{c}{-16%}	\multicolumn{2}{c}{-19%}	\multicolumn{2}{c}{-4%}	\multicolumn{2}{c}{-23%}	\multicolumn{2}{c}{n/a}

Source: National Science Foundation CASPAR Database System.

While many private schools are able to offset declining revenue income by strengthening endowment earnings, the Coalition schools typically generate inconsequential income from this source. Indeed, compared to the national private four-year college average for the share of revenue coming from endowment of 5%, the Coalition school average has hovered at 3% since the early 1980s (see Table 20). On the positive side, a number of schools with virtually no endowment funds in 1981 have made small progress over the past decade, thus accounting for an overall positive change in this ratio of 136%. Not surprisingly, Improving colleges experienced the largest average gain (214%).

Table 20. **Change in Financial Ratio: Endowment Income to Total E & G Revenues by Group 1981 to 1991**

	\multicolumn{8}{c}{CCCU Schools}	All 4-year Privates	
	All 81	All 91	Improving 81	Improving 91	Stable 81	Stable 91	Declining 81	Declining 91	81	91
Mean Ratio	0.03	0.03	0.03	0.03	0.04	0.04	0.02	0.03	0.05	0.05
Range - Min.	0.00	0.00	0.00	0.00	0.00	0.00	0.00	0.00	n/a	n/a
Max.	0.22	0.13	0.13	0.10	0.22	0.09	0.10	0.13	n/a	n/a
Mean % Change 1981 - 1991	\multicolumn{2}{c}{136%}	\multicolumn{2}{c}{214%}	\multicolumn{2}{c}{92%}	\multicolumn{2}{c}{88%}	\multicolumn{2}{c}{n/a}

Source: National Science Foundation CASPAR Database System.

In assessing change in financial condition it is helpful to examine whether specific areas of the institution are getting a growing or dwindling share of the total available revenues. This can be especially helpful in looking for reasons expenditures are outpacing revenue. In the case of the Coalition schools, Table 21 provides some useful data. As shown here, the percentage of revenue income being used to support the academic programs of the institution has increased only slightly between 1981 and 1991 while the percentage of revenue being siphoned off to support student scholarship programs increased significantly. Indeed, the schools spend slightly less of their revenue income on instruction than the national average while spending significantly more on scholarships and grants. For both categories, the change is most significant for Improving colleges. The Improving colleges in the aggregate decreased the percentage of revenue going to support instruction and currently commit a lower percentage to this function than do either the Stable or Declining colleges.

Table 21. **Change in Financial Ratio: Instructional Expenditures to Total E & G Revenues by Group 1981 to 1991**

CCCU Schools

	All 81	All 91	Improving 81	Improving 91	Stable 81	Stable 91	Declining 81	Declining 91	All 4-year Privates 81	All 4-year Privates 91
Mean Ratio	0.25	0.24	0.24	0.23	0.25	0.26	0.25	0.25	0.26	0.26
Range - Min.	0.11	0.13	0.11	0.13	0.17	0.15	0.17	0.17	n/a	n/a
Max.	0.38	0.35	0.32	0.35	0.38	0.35	0.37	0.33	n/a	n/a
Mean % Change 1981 - 1991	0.01%		0.00%		0.03%		0.00%		n/a	

Change in Financial Ratio: Scholarship Expenditures to Total E & G Revenues by Group 1981 to 1991

CCCU Schools

	All 81	All 91	Improving 81	Improving 91	Stable 81	Stable 91	Declining 81	Declining 91	All 4-year Privates 81	All 4-year Privates 91
Mean Ratio	0.09	0.15	0.09	0.15	0.08	0.13	0.10	0.15	0.06	0.09
Range - Min.	0.01	0.05	0.01	0.05	0.02	0.07	0.02	0.08	n/a	n/a
Max.	0.27	0.25	0.19	0.25	0.18	0.20	0.27	0.25	n/a	n/a
Mean % Change 1981 - 1991	130%		186%		105%		91%		n/a	

Source: National Science Foundation CASPAR Database System.

The percentage of revenue income being used to support the academic programs of the institution has increased only slightly between 1981 and 1991 while the percentage of revenue being siphoned off to support student scholarship programs increased significantly.

Regarding the scholarship category, Improving colleges commit a higher percentage of their revenue income to support student scholarships, followed closely by Declining and Stable colleges. It is interesting to speculate about the possibility of a relationship between increased scholarship and grant-in-aid assistance offered by the Improving colleges and the increased enrollment these schools have experienced over the same period. Clearly, this could be one explanation for why the Improving colleges, despite increasing enrollments, appear by some financial measures to be in no better or only slightly better financial health than either the Stable or Declining colleges.

A final ratio which is frequently used to assess an institution's overall financial strength is the ratio of available assets to general liabilities. In brief, this ratio gives an indication of the institution's ability to meet its most pressing debts, or, in other words, the amount of "cushion" available for debt coverage. Analysts suggest that as long as debt is outstanding, available assets should be at least twice as great as general liabilities, thus making 2.0:1 the minimum threshold for this ratio. Using this as a guideline for assessment, the Coalition schools in the aggregate appear to be in better shape on this ratio in 1991 than in 1981. As shown in Table 22, 29 of the Coalition schools meet this threshold in 1991, compared to only ten in 1981. The greatest increase has come among the Improving colleges (aggregate increase of 784%), followed by the Stable colleges (aggregate increase of 366%) and the Declining colleges (aggre-

Table 22. **Change in Financial Ratio: Total Assets to Total Liabilities by Group 1981 to 1991**

	All 81	All 91	Improving 81	Improving 91	Stable 81	Stable 91	Declining 81	Declining 91
Mean Ratio	19.08	4.91	0.65	3.14	2.21	7.58	51.43	4.66
Range - Min.	-0.56	-1.31	-0.56	-0.19	0.03	0.21	-0.11	-1.31
Max.	1395.00	95.82	4.05	15.36	16.23	95.82	1395.00	54.20
Mean % Change	439%		784%		366%		131%	
Number of Schools With Ratios:								
(.500) and below	1	2	1	0	0	0	0	2
(.001)-(.499)	6	2	5	1	0	0	1	1
.001-.999	51	24	17	7	17	8	17	9
1.00-1.99	12	23	3	11	2	5	7	7
2.00-2.99	3	6	1	3	2	2	0	1
3.00-3.99	1	2	0	0	1	0	0	2
4.00-4.99	1	6	1	2	0	2	0	2
5.00 and up	5	15	0	4	2	7	3	4

Source: National Science Foundation CASPAR Database System.

gate increase of 131%). The mean ratio for each group provides a slightly different picture. While the Improving colleges currently have the lowest mean ratio (3.1 versus 7.5 and 4.6), the colleges in this group have clearly made the biggest gains in building a debt coverage cushion. On the other hand, as Table 21 illustrates, the Declining colleges lost significant ground during this same period.

Summary

The demographic and financial variables examined and described above yield findings which are consistent with previously conducted studies as well as findings which are contradictory to previous work in this field. A number of these findings are worth repeating.

Despite a declining national high school graduating pool, Coalition schools in the aggregate outpaced other four-year private colleges in undergraduate and FTE enrollment growth during the 1980s. At the same time, graduate enrollment increased at Coalition schools on average by 25% during the 1980s. The number of schools offering at least one graduate program jumped from 21 in 1981 to 40 in 1991. The greatest gains have come among the Improving colleges where the number of schools offering at least one program jumped from 7 to 15 during the 1980s.

Freshmen headcount and admissions trends among the Coalition schools provide a more disconcerting picture regarding the current condition of the sector. Clearly, and especially for Declining and Stable colleges, institutional enrollment shortfalls during the 1980s appear to be attributable in large part to a declining traditional freshman population. On the positive side and in contrast to national norms, the new student acceptance rate at Coalition schools decreased an average of 7% during the 1980s (this compares to a national average increase of 3%), suggesting a tightening of academic standards. Nevertheless, Coalition schools are still accepting an uncomfortably high percentage of applicants (81% versus a national norm of 63%). And, there is a sharp increase across all three groups in the number of provisionally accepted freshmen and the number of new students needing remediation.

A number of external factors as well as inherent institutional characteristics appear to play a role in the differing conditions experienced by Coalition institutions over the past decade. For example, Improving and Stable colleges are more likely than Declining colleges to be located in less populated areas, suggesting that environmental setting may play a greater role in the

> While there are important differences across the sector, and while many Coalition schools do appear to be making some positive gains on several of these measures, one is nevertheless left with the sense that the sector as a whole emerged from the 1980s in a profoundly weakened financial state.

well-being of this kind of institution than has been found in other studies. On the other hand, Declining colleges are more likely to be located in urban settings and in regions of the country which experienced the sharpest decline in the number of high school graduates during the 1980s (Northeast and North-central), suggesting that geographic location may also contribute in some way to the deteriorating condition of these schools. Two other institutional characteristics are notable: 1) Improving colleges in this study consistently enrolled a significantly higher percentage of in-state students than Stable or Declining colleges. This contradicts previous research which suggested a positive relationship between a national student drawing market and enrollment growth. 2) Improving colleges in this study experienced sharper increases in the percentage of the student body residing on the campus than the Stable or Declining colleges. Taken together, these findings suggest that administrators should consider the potential impact of external or inherent institutional factors upon their efforts toward resiliency.

Finally, despite growing enrollments, the Coalition schools appear to have very limited and in some cases, clearly inadequate, financial resource bases. For example, in 1991, no school met the minimum threshold for the ratio of expendable fund balances to plant debt. Only a handful of the schools met the minimum threshold for the ratio of total assets to total liabilities. Given the dearth of current, national ratio benchmarks, and the fact that the threshold suggested in the literature is a "theoretical ideal," some caution should be taken in the interpretation of this finding. Nevertheless, the net-to-total revenue trend lines suggest that, even at those schools experiencing some enrollment and tuition revenue growth, expenses are increasing at a rate greater than what revenue will support. In short, many of these schools appear to have dwindling financial reserves. This can be explained in part by the fact that Coalition schools have grown increasingly dependent upon tuition income (as other revenue sources, e.g., private gift and endowment earnings have decreased or stayed flat) while siphoning off ever greater shares of revenue to support spiraling financial aid expenses.

While there are important differences across the sector, and while many Coalition schools do appear to be making some positive gains on several of these measures, one is nevertheless left with the sense that the sector as a whole emerged from the 1980s in a profoundly weakened financial state. These measures, coupled with the open-ended survey responses, suggest that the most pressing priorities for the majority of these institutions include the following: 1) strengthening financial reserves; 2) strengthening revenue generation efforts; 3) controlling financial aid spending (without negatively impacting enrollment), and 4) implementing a balanced financial management approach, (i.e., one that involves both selective pruning and investment of resources).

CHAPTER THREE

A Framework for Understanding Institutional Resiliency

A Framework for Understanding Institutional Resiliency

A growing body of literature has evolved since the 1970s which provides a comprehensive framework for understanding the various responses to institutional adversity and the reasons for institutional demise and/or resiliency. This literature base borrows heavily from the business management and organizational theory fields, as well as from higher education research. While there is considerable overlap, this base can be divided into three distinct clusters: 1) organizational adaptation literature; 2) strategic planning and business management literature, and 3) successful college management literature. In this chapter, those concepts and findings of most relevance to the Christian college and university sector are reviewed.

Organizational Adaptation Literature

The body of organizational adaptation literature is quite new (most has been published since the 1970s) and draws heavily from the fields of sociology and business. Cameron (1984) provides a definition for the concept of "organizational adaptation" which seems to encompass most of the research in the field:

> *Organizational adaptation refers to modifications and alterations in the organization or its components in order to adjust to changes in the external environment. Its purpose is to restore equilibrium to an imbalanced condition. Organizational adaptation generally refers to a process, not an event, whereby changes are instituted in organizations. Adaptation does not necessarily imply reactivity on the part of an organization because proactive or anticipatory adaptation is possible as well. But the emphasis is definitely on responding to some discontinuity or lack of fit that arises between the organization and its environment (p. 123).*

Figure 3 illustrates the various approaches to organizational adaptation taken by researchers working in the field. These approaches can be divided into four general categories, ranging from those assuming little or no managerial influence but significant environmental power to those assuming substantial managerial discretion with a less prominent role for the external environment.

Organizational adaptation refers to modifications and alterations in the organization or its components in order to adjust to changes in the external environment. Its purpose is to restore equilibrium to an imbalanced condition.

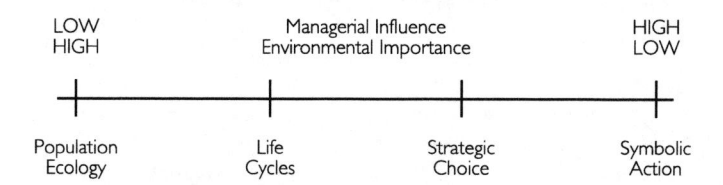

Figure 3. **Categories of Approaches to Organizational Adaptation**

```
LOW              Managerial Influence              HIGH
HIGH             Environmental Importance          LOW
+----------------+----------------+----------------+
Population       Life             Strategic        Symbolic
Ecology          Cycles           Choice           Action
```

Source: K.S. Cameron in "Organizational Adaptation and Higher Education," Journal of Higher Education, 55 (no. 2), 122-144.

    The "population ecology" or "natural selection" view reflects the ideas of those researchers who view the environment as a powerful and pervasive force (Aldrich, 1979; Aldrich & Pfeffer, 1976; Birnbaum, 1983; Hannan & Freeman, 1977; McKelvey, 1982). According to these authors, adaptation occurs not because of intelligent or creative managerial action, but instead by the random and evolutionary development of characteristics that are compatible with the environment. Essentially, managerial discretion and influence are neither present nor relevant. Instead, the environment selects out those organizational forms most likely to survive (the "fittest" species are those forms with characteristics most in sync with the environment) while all other forms die out.

    Basic to this perspective is the idea that adaptation is meaningful only if it is viewed from the population level of analysis—the only meaningful change occurs as major shifts among entire populations of organizations, not as minor adjustments in existing organizational forms. To illustrate, a population ecologist would likely view the existence in the environment of a large number of middle-class, career-oriented high school graduates interested in nonresidential, low-cost educational opportunities, coupled with general public support for higher education, as important stimuli for the phenomenal growth which has taken place in recent years in the public community college and regional state university sectors. Likewise, the same environmental factors would be viewed as culprits in the decline and near demise over the last half century of the private junior college sector.

    A somewhat less deterministic approach, the "life cycles" perspective, also emphasizes the notion of evolutionary change and the powerful role of the environment but allows for more managerial discretion. According to the proponents of this view (Cameron & Whetten, 1981; Quinn & Cameron, 1983), the

> The administrators at declining schools were more concerned with resource allocation than resource generation and were inclined to be more concerned about "doing things right" while the emphases of administrators at growing institutions were just the opposite.

single organization is the preferred unit of analysis. Organizations are assumed to progress through at least four sequential developmental stages: 1) creativity and entrepreneurship; 2) collectivity; 3) formalization and control, and 4) elaboration and structure (p. 525). At each stage, unique organizational features develop to enable the organization to overcome a set of commonly occurring problems. These problems are overcome by successfully progressing on to the next life-cycle stage. Without direct managerial intervention to alter this natural evolutionary process, organizational adaptation tends to follow a predictable sequence. Two assumptions differentiating this perspective from the first are that managers can speed up, slow down, or even abort the sequential development by their actions, and that a recycling process begins to happen after the final stage has been reached. In essence, managerial action as well as features distinct to each organization help determine to which stage the organization ultimately returns.

On the other end of the continuum are two categories of approaches assuming substantial managerial influence. The proponents of these perspectives suggest that organizations are not at the mercy of an unchangeable environment but can act to influence the environment. While the literature base supporting the notion that organizational adaptation results from managerial action is quite diverse, it can be categorized into two thematic-type models: the strategic choice and symbolic action perspectives. The "strategic choice" perspective subsumes a number of similar approaches, the most prominent of which include the resource-dependence model (Pfeffer & Salancik, 1978), the political-economy model (Wamsley & Zald, 1973), and the strategy-structure model (Chandler, 1962). While the advocates of this approach recognize the importance of external environmental influences and the need for a fit between these influences and the organization's structure and process, more emphasis is placed upon the availability of a variety of strategies which enables managers to modify their environments and subsequently determine the success or failure of the adaptation process (Aldrich & Pfeffer, 1979; Child, 1972).

Examples of "strategic choice"-related research include a major study involving the tobacco industry in which Miles and Cameron (1982) found that organizations adapt successfully to turbulent and hostile environments by implementing three types of strategies in sequence: 1) domain defense strategies (designed to enhance the legitimacy of the organization and buffer it from environmental encroachment); 2) domain offense strategies (designed to expand the organization in its current areas of expertise as well as to exploit environmental weaknesses), and 3) domain creation strategies (designed to minimize risk by diversifying into safer or less turbulent areas of the environment).

A second study conducted by Miles and Snow (1978) found that successful organizations develop a particular orientation (or a strategic competence) that enables the implementation of a specific set of strategies at different times and in different ways. These strategic orientations include "prospectors" (innovative organizations: first in their field to implement new strategies), "analyzers" (organizations that typically wait for evidence regarding a strategy's success before implementing), "defenders" (slow-adapting organizations: typi-cally seeking stability), and "reactors" (organizations typically unable to follow through with any kind of consistent adaptive response:strategies implemented sporadically). Miles and Snow (1978) as well as other researchers (Snow & Hrebiniak, 1980) have found empirical evidence linking these orientations to effective organizational adaptation under varying environmental conditions. In general, "reacting" organizations adapt least effectively while the other types adapt more or less successfully depending upon a host of influencing factors.

The final perspective, the "symbolic action" approach, assumes a significantly less prominent role for the external environment than the other three views. Instead, this model assumes that managers enjoy significant influence to change their external environments and to change the organization's response to those environments. Advocates of this approach focus on change in symbols, interpretations, and stories as opposed to change in structure or technology. According to researchers working within this paradigm, organizational adaptation comes about through the use of a variety of strategies involving language, ritual, and symbolic behavior designed to modify organizational members' shared meanings. Weick (1976) has termed this process "enacting the external environment" and cites the following as powerful managerial tools for managing change: interpreting history and current events, using rituals or ceremonies, using time or measurement, redesigning physical space, and introducing doubt.

Cameron (1984) is one of the few organizational adaptation theorists to extend his work to the field of higher education. In a study of 40 colleges and universities representing a wide range of institutional type, Cameron attempted to determine the reasons why some schools declined in enrollment, why others grew, and why some experienced little to no change in enrollment over a six-year period. Of the three groups, Cameron found that declining colleges were most distinct in their response patterns. Specifically, he found that declining colleges used more standardized structures and relied more heavily on conservative practices which had worked in the past. The declining schools viewed the external environment as being lean in resources and gave themselves lower ratings with regard to academic effectiveness and morale. At the same time, the declining schools yielded higher effectiveness ratings with regard to internal organizational concerns such as efficiency and fiscal and budgeting matters.

Interestingly, the most significant differences among declining, improving, and stable colleges occurred in the strategic emphasis of senior administrators. For example, in declining colleges, administrators gave greater emphasis to budgeting, fiscal, and fundraising concerns and less attention to strengthening relations with external constituencies. The administrators at declining schools were more concerned with resource allocation than resource generation and were inclined to be more concerned about "doing things right" while the emphases of administrators at growing institutions were just the opposite. At the growing schools, considerable emphasis was placed upon interacting with external constituencies, with strengthening public relations and service functions, with acquiring new resources, and with "doing the right things."

Cameron's findings are supported by several other studies (Cyert, 1980; Hedberg, Nystrom & Starbuck, 1976; Weick, 1976) which have suggested that "self-designing" characteristics (e.g., innovation, fluidity, adaptability to external factors) are the most appropriate prescriptions for organizations facing decline. In particular, Cyert (1980) proposes that the actions which are engendered from "self-designing" characteristics are essential for breaking the vicious cycle in which declining organizations often find themselves (e.g., a college experiences fiscal problems due to enrollment decline and then raises tuition to counter the fiscal distress only to further accelerate the enrollment drop-off). Cyert and others conclude that the constant nurturing of innovation and flow of new ideas, the expanding of resources bases, and the nurturing of contacts with the external environment are important actions for organizations seeking to maintain and/or strengthen their viability.

In summarizing these diverse views on organizational adaptation, Cameron (1984) suggests that the postindustrial environment in which higher education is now situated demands a radically new way of thinking and managing on the part of administrators. Indeed, he argues that to assure survival, strength, and soundness during these increasingly turbulent and complex times, higher education administrators need to become

Janusian[1] thinkers and develop Janusian institutions. According to Cameron, *Janusian* thinking occurs when "two contradictory thoughts are held to be true simultaneously—the explanation or resolution of the contradiction is what leads to major breakthroughs in insight" (1984, p. 293). Moreover, holding such apparently contradictory thoughts enables the flexibility of thought that is a prerequisite for individual creativity and problem solving. Cameron suggests that perpetuating Janusian characteristics in institutions also has the effect of producing flexibility and adaptability, and it enables organizations to cope better with unpredictable environments. Among the Janusian characteristics identified by Cameron as being most essential for institutional survival during turbulent times are the following: 1) the simultaneous nurturing of loosely and tightly coupled systems[2]; 2) the bolstering of both stability and flexibility; 3) a wider search for information as well as mechanisms to inhibit information overload; 4) the nurturing of both consensus and heterogeneity in decision making; 5) proactivity and reactivity in strategic decision making, and 6) continuity of leadership and the infusion of new leaders with new ideas.

Interestingly, *Janusian* thinking is very similar to what Peters and Waterman (1982), in their now classic work, *In Search of Excellence*, identify as "loose-tight properties." In the excellent organizations profiled, the authors observe that while each organization exhibited an almost fanatical commitment to mission and shared values, employees were given tremendous freedom and flexibility to use their creativity and talents in fulfilling that mission. Consequently, these organizations bred cultures which were both highly focused on mission and ideology and at the same time intensely opportunistic and innovative. In a more recent study which examined the habits and behaviors of 18 exceptional and long-lasting companies, Collins and Porras (1994) found that one of the most significant factors differentiating these companies from the competition was the presence of this paradoxical focus: these truly exceptional companies were focused concurrently on "preserving a tightly held core ideology and stimulating vigorous change and movement, on nurturing a clear vision and sense of direction and opportunistic groping and experimentation, and on maintaining both ideological control and operational autonomy" (p. 44).

"To assure survival, strength, and soundness during these increasingly turbulent and complex times, higher education administrators need to become Janusian thinkers and develop Janusian institutions" (Cameron, 1984).

---

[1] *The concept of Janusian thinking was first introduced by Rothenburg (1979) while investigating the creative accomplishments of such geniuses as Einstein, Mozart, Picasso, and O'Neill. The term comes from Roman mythology and is named for the Roman god, Janus, whose two heads faced in opposite directions at the same time.*

[2] *A loosely coupled system is one where connections among elements are weak, indirect, occasional, negligible, or discontinuous, while tightly coupled systems are controlled and coordinated so as to achieve specified goals.*

Strategic Planning and Management Literature

The second literature base is defined broadly and includes research which draws from the strategic planning and management areas. While the term strategic planning first arose in a military context dating back to ancient Greece, the concept did not come into prominence in business circles until the publication of Chandler's 1962 classic, Strategy and Structure. "Strategic management" was brought into the lexicon with the publication of Ansoff and Hayes' 1976 classic, From Strategic Planning to Strategic Management. This work was instrumental in encouraging a shift away from strategic planning to strategic management. Viewing the former as too limiting (e.g., the outcome of planning being confined merely to a set of plans and intentions), Ansoff and Hayes and others advocated for a broader-based, more integrative approach to managing change. According to Ansoff and Hayes, strategic management includes the operational management of the organization's competitive mode ("planning"), the entrepreneurial management of the organization's entrepreneurial mode ("adapting"), and the integrative management of both modes ("planned learning"). Chaffee (1985) echoes this thinking in her more recent definition of strategic management as "a complex socio-dynamic process for strategic change which goes beyond planning to include entrepreneurial management and its integration with planning" (p. 134).

By the early 1980s, the concept of strategic management had taken such a hold in the business literature that some declared strategic planning to be a "dead idea" (e.g., Ginter & White, 1982, p. 253; Jemison, 1981, p. 637). The concept of strategy was borrowed from business by higher education; however, higher education's use of the concept has significantly lagged behind the business world. Consequently, much of the higher education literature still emphasizes the notion of strategic planning—higher education has yet to catch up with the shift to strategic management.

Despite its limitations, strategic planning can provide help for colleges seeking to survive these turbulent times. According to several observers (Chaffee, 1985; Cope, 1981; Kotler & Murphy, 1981; Shirley, 1983), strategic planning offers particular benefit for liberal arts colleges seeking a better fit between organizational features and the changing external environment. In brief, strategic planning helps to raise awareness of the institution's internal and external environments, focuses the decision-making process on actions most critical to the

The truly exceptional companies were focused concurrently on "preserving a tightly held core ideology and stimulating vigorous change and movement, on nurturing a clear vision and sense of direction and opportunistic groping and experimentation, and on maintaining both ideological control and operational autonomy" (Collins & Porras, 1994).

Survival Strategies for Christian Colleges and Universities

institution's survival in the current market, and encourages futuristic scanning and possibility thinking, resulting in critical actions taken today in anticipation of tomorrow's market needs (Chaffee, 1985).

Because the range of strategic options is narrower in higher education than in business (due in great part to the distinctive character of academic organizations), there is a significant void in the literature regarding the meaning and definition of strategy and how strategy works in a college or university setting. Higher education researchers have only recently begun empirical studies to explore the nature of adaptive strategy and its linkage to higher education performance. Moreover, Chaffee (1985) suggests that those using the term strategy, be they in business or higher education, generally believe they are working with a uni-dimensional model, whereas her review of the literature suggests that strategy is both multidimensional and situational. Indeed, Chaffee's work suggests three distinguishable models of strategy which, when taken together, constitute a strategic management approach.

According to Chaffee, each model (see Table 23) describes a set of organizational functions or behaviors for which the term "strategy" has typically been applied in the literature. The first model, "linear strategy," refers to such topics as organizational goals, rational planning, program review, priority setting, master planning and forecasting. Essentially, this model is premised on the assumption that leaders can plan rationally as to how to best deal with their competitors to achieve organizational goals. The second model, "adaptive strategy," is premised on the belief that organizations exist to acquire and retain resources. Higher education strategies which reflect an adaptive approach include conducting marketing research, changing programs or adding new majors in response to market needs, conserving operating funds, and making changes to attract students. In contrast, according to the third model, "interpretive strategy," the most fundamental organizational issues involve the improvement and enhancement of credibility and legitimacy. Higher education strategies which reflect this latter approach include refining and/or reaffirming the mission, strengthening institutional communication channels, undertaking initiatives with external constituencies, and improving the institution's image. Most of the research dealing with strategy in higher education expresses the "adaptive" model (e.g., Cope, 1981; Keller, 1983; Peterson, 1980).

Chaffee used this framework in an attempt to explain why some private colleges rebound more resiliently and fully than others from a period of financial decline. Essentially, she looked at the behaviors and subsequent situations of two sets of private

Table 23. **A Comparison of the Adaptive and Interpretive Models of Strategic Management**

	Adaptive	*Interpretive*
Nature of the Organization:	Entity, Organism	Social Contract
Nature of Organizational Action:	Substantive	Symbolic
Fundamental Requirement of the Organization:	Resources	Legitimacy
Fundamental Organizational Issue:	What are we Doing?	Why are we Together?
Focus for Strategy:	Means	Participants and Potential Organizational Participants
Trigger for Change in Strategy:	Resource Crisis; Change in External Demand	Credibility Crisis
Nature of Strategic Action:	Change Products/Services; Diversify & Anticipate Markets; Create Organizational Slack	Develop Symbols/Concepts; Improve Communication with Key Groups and Individuals
Aims of Strategic Action:	Coalign Organization with Environment; Acquire Resources	Legitimacy; Credibility Improvement

Source: E.E. Chaffee, "Successful Strategic Management in Small Private Colleges," Journal of Higher Education, 55 (No. 2, 1984): 212-241.

colleges experiencing severe financial difficulties in the mid-1970s. She divided the sample into two subsets: 1) those in a better position in 1982 than before decline, and 2) those not in a better position. In comparing the strategic responses of both groups, Chaffee found that while the "adaptive" model was followed by most members of both groups, the "interpretive" model was followed consistently by the more resilient colleges to a greater extent than the less resilient colleges. In brief, while the "adaptive" model appeared to assist colleges in their recovery efforts, it was not useful in accounting for faster recovery of the more resilient group. The "interpretive" model, on the other hand, seems to have facilitated a more rapid recovery. Chaffee notes that a frequent assumption made by college leaders is that actions such as changing academic programs and attending to recruitment are primary levers for improving institutional condition. However, her study reveals that while both the declining and improving colleges did these things, there were other important considerations: 1) changing academic programs in response to decline may be unnecessary and even harmful; other actions may be the key to recovery; 2) adaptive strategies may be successfully implemented and still not lead to enduring solutions; 3) changes expressing interpretive strategy are likely to be highly effective; changes contradictory or irrelevant to interpretive strategy may be more costly than beneficial, and 4) identifying the primary levers for improving the condition of a college is a function intrinsic to the college and can only be performed with reference to that specific college; in other words, effective turnaround strategy is unique to the context of each institution.

Based on her findings, Chaffee offered several recommendations for colleges seeking guidance on how to enhance their conditions: 1) the establishment of an interpretive strategy that guides the adaptive strategy is preferable to using only adaptive strategy; 2) the establishment of an interpretive strategy requires a strong and clear sense of organizational identity, as well as a willingness to make decisions based on that identity; 3) presidents who base their actions on symbolic as well as substantive concerns will be more effective turnaround leaders than those who ignore the symbolic implications of organizational life; 4) colleges have a wide range of strategic moves that they might productively make, and 5) the specific components of effective turnaround strategy evolve from and are unique to the institution.

Successful College Management Literature

The third body of literature consists of a number of works written in the 1970s and 1980s under the rubric of successful college management practices. In response to the cries of impending doom beginning as early as 1970, a multitude of books and articles appeared on the higher education landscape. In general, the literature includes analyses of the difficulties facing academe, as well as suggestions for restoring and ensuring institutional vitality. Table 24 provides a summary of the factors identified in the research as having importance for efforts toward institutional resiliency. Taken together, these works provide a rich source of suggestions for institutions seeking to effectively adapt to the assorted complexities of the 1980s and 1990s.

There appears to be a split in the research between those who believe that college decline and/or growth is due primarily to external factors and those who attribute a changing condition to internal institutional factors which are within management's control. One study (Cohen, 1983), conducted specifically to examine the impact of the external environment on enrollment growth or decline, looked at colleges which had been successful in reversing a declining enrollment trend and compared these schools to a control group of colleges which had not been successful in reversing decline. Cohen found that external variables were generally more important than internal response strategies for explaining enrollment growth or decline. Specifically, six of nine external variables tested were found to be statistically significant at or above a .05 level including demographic changes

In comparing the strategic responses of both groups, Chaffee found that while the "adaptive" model was followed by most members of both groups, the "interpretive" model was followed consistently by the more resilient colleges to a greater extent than the less resilient colleges.

Table 24. **Summary of Successful College Management Research Findings: Factors Influencing Institutional Resiliency and Decline**

Factors Influencing Resiliency:	Authors:
Adoption of revenue-generating management emphasis	St. John (1991); Peck (1984); Hamlin & Hungerford (1988); Mingle & Norris (1981)
Bold, entrepreneurial, visionary presidential leadership style	St. John (1991); Peck (1984); Hamlin & Hungerford (1988); Mingle & Norris (1981)
Strengthening academic standards	Mingle & Norris (1981)
Addition or expansion in academic program offerings	Cohen (1983); Buffington (1990)
Employment of a "strategic" management approach (e.g., market-driven, opportunity-conscious, innovative, creative, selective pruning coupled with "high potential" expansion)	Parker (1987); Cyert (1978); Cameron (1984); Chaffee (1984); Peck (1984); Hambrick & Schecter (1983)
Change in level of degree programs offered	Cohen (1983)
Strengthening quality and diversity of academic programs	St. John (1991); Breneman (1983); Zammuto (1983)
Competitive tuition pricing	St. John (1991); Peck (1984); Parker (1987); Breneman (1983)
Institutional size (<1,000)	Hilpert (1987); Tempel (1985); Carnegie (1975)
Strong image and sense of prestige	Breneman (1983); Zammuto (1983)
Wide mission consensus and sense of clarity	St. John (1991); Peck (1984); Parker (1987); Brenman (1983)
Primarily national student recruitment pool	Breneman (1983); Zammuto (1983)
Urban location	Breneman (1983); Tempel (1985); Mingle & Norris (1981)
Primarily in-state student recruitment pool	Buffington (1990)
Caring and supportive campus ethos	Buffington (1990); Mingle & Norris (1981)
Improved student retention	Mingle & Norris (1981); Tempel (1985)
Adoption of a comprehensive enrollment management approach	St. John (1991)
Well-run organization (operationally)	Peck (1984); St. John (1991)
Changed missions	Carnegie (1975); Tempel (1985); King (1981)
Healthy financial condition	Tempel (1985); Carnegie (1975)
Strengthening of student life programs	Tempel (1985); Mingle & Norris (1981)
Broadened recruitment focus	Tempel (1985); Carnegie (1975)
Increased fundraising activity	Tempel (1985); King (1981); Mingle & Norris (1981)
Increased recruitment activity	Tempel (1985); King (1981); Mingle & Norris (1981)
Implemented selective cut-backs	Carnegie (1975); King (1981); Mingle & Norris (1981)

Factors Influencing Decline:	Authors:
Lack of breadth in program offerings	Zammuto (1983); Breneman (1983)
Limited student recruitment market drawing area (i.e., within state)	Hilpert (1987)
Institutional size (>1,000)	Hilpert (1987); Tempel (1985)
Minimal endowment	Jonson (1984)
Declining high school graduating pool	Mingle & Norris (1981)
Increased competition	Mingle & Norris (1981)
Federal and state policy changes	Mingle & Norris (1981)
Insufficient financial base	Jonson (1984)
Presence of multiple financial distress indicators (e.g., expenses consistently outpacing revenues; high tuition dependency, high ratios of student aid as % of revenue income)	Jonson (1984)
Failure in top management/leadership	Jonson (1984)
Over-emphasis on efficiency measures (i.e., conserving resources)	Rubin (1977)
Non-competitive tuition pricing	Cohen (1983); Hilpert (1987)
Weakened admissions standards	Cohen (1983); Breneman (1987)
Lack of missional or institutional distinctiveness	Jonson (1984); Parker (1987); Zammuto (1983)
Lack of clarity about mission	Parker (1987)

in the potential pool of high school graduates and changes in job market conditions in the state in which the college is located. The only internal responses found to have any significance included the introduction of new or expanded academic programs and a change in the level of academic degree programs offered (i.e., going from bachelors- to masters-granting level). Cohen found two institutional response strategies which were counterproductive in dealing with enrollment decline: 1) increasing tuition and fees, and 2) lowering the standards for admissions application acceptances. Cohen concluded somewhat skeptically that the ability of a college or university to reverse enrollment decline is predominately a function of variables external to the institution, and that reversal of enrollment decline is generally not responsive to "managerial heroics."

Breneman (1983) identified several factors affecting an institution's ability to weather an increasingly turbulent environment and found that a mix of internal and external factors accounted for heightened institutional resiliency: 1) quality and diversity of program offerings; 2) institutional location; 3) institutional image and sense of prestige vis-à-vis the competition; 4) institutional price vis-à-vis the competition, and 5) recruitment practices and policies.

In his now classic work on decline among colleges and universities in the 1970s, Zammuto (1983) uncovered similar findings. Specifically, Zammuto found that a lack of mission or institutional distinctiveness, lack of breadth in program offerings, and a limited market drawing area increase vulnerability to external conditions of decline. According to Zammuto, the more limited a college's program offerings, the less flexibility it has to adapt quickly to shifting student interests. For example, the declining interest in teacher education in the 1970s left many small liberal arts colleges with over-staffed education faculties, empty classrooms, and insufficient flexibility for a shift in focus. Zammuto also found that colleges drawing their students from national markets or broadly defined regional markets (500 plus miles away from the campus) tended to be less vulnerable to decline. Schools drawing their students primarily from within state were more susceptible to local economic and demographic trends.

In a follow-up study, Zammuto (1986) examined a group of colleges over a ten year period 1971 to 1981 in an attempt to explain the phenomenon of decline. Zammuto used enrollment and revenue trends over the ten-year period to categorize institutions into three groups: Growing, Declining, and Stable colleges. At the conclusion of his study, Zammuto offered three observations: 1) there was a decreasing percentage of colleges experiencing both growing enrollment and growing revenue, suggesting a more scarce universe; 2) there was significant variation in the incidence of growth and/or decline, suggesting that factors other than the size of the traditional 18-22 year old cohort has a large impact on enrollment growth, and 3) given this variety, it is impossible to specify "cookbook" management techniques which are applicable to all institutions.

Like Cameron, Zammuto cautions that the processes for managing decline and growth are distinctly different and suggests that colleges that most effectively deal with decline do the following: 1) focus on achieving a clear understanding of and consensus about mission; 2) assess continually the institutional enrollment flow and identify those places likely to yield the highest pay-off; 3) assess continually the institution's environment, including the specific enrollment pool from which the institution draws students; 4) engage in ongoing program review and updating; 5) engage in contingency planning, and 6) maintain control of any cut-back processes by employing selective cuts and reallocating resources to support new and strategic initiatives.

Tempel's 1985 study, which described and analyzed the response patterns of small, less-selective liberal arts colleges to conditions of scarcity (i.e., a declining enrollment pool and decreasing financial resources) during the early 1980s, yielded results suggesting that external factors were largely responsible for decline and/or growth. In brief, Tempel found that: 1) enrollment size played a significant role in an institution's ability to launch an effective response to scarcity, e.g., larger institutions were more able to develop aggressive program expansion and financial development activity; 2) healthy institutions became healthier, and 3) urban institutions were in better enrollment and financial health than institutions located in less densely populated areas. Of the 25 internal and external factors examined in Tempel's study, only size and location exhibited significantly strong relationships with incidences of growth and/or decline. Likewise, Hilpert (1987) found that the type of college most vulnerable to enrollment decline tended to be small in size, under sectarian control, have a student body drawn from a narrowly defined region (such as within the state), have higher-than-average tuition levels, and a minimal endowment base.

In a more recent study, Buffington (1990) found that inherent institutional characteristics and actions played a pivotal role in influencing institutional condition. For example, Buffington surveyed 55 moderately selective liberal arts colleges in order to identify which enrollment management strategies were most helpful to increasing enrollment. In general, enrollment-increasing colleges reported higher usage of innovative-type strategies (expanding course offerings), while maintaining colleges ranked higher on strategies pertaining to distinctive character, mission, and concern for students. Declining colleges ranked higher on strategies dealing directly with admissions efforts. Two strategies in statistically greater use at the increasing colleges included expanding days and times of courses and using outcome studies in the development of new programs. Declining colleges were statistically more likely to consider enrollment concerns a priority and to have hired an enrollment consultant.

Buffington's study also involved testing Chaffee's strategic management typology. Here she found that interpretive strategies were used more frequently than adaptive strategies across all three groups of colleges and that enrollment-increasing colleges used adaptive strategy more frequently than did decreasing or maintaining institutions. Buffington also found that some of the major contributors to enrollment change seemed to be inherent institutional characteristics such as percentage of in-state students and number of academic programs offered. She found little correlation between enrollment success and the use of specific strategies; however, those institutions engaging in multiple strategies and using them frequently seemed to achieve greater success than those institutions using them less frequently. Also, for these colleges, a campus ethos which promoted a sense of care and concern for the individual seemed to have a positive impact on enrollment.

In a study of 20 colleges in 11 southern states, Mingle and Norris (1981) found that a combination of external and internal factors accounted for declining enrollments during the 1970s. External factors facilitating decline included the declining high school graduating pool, increased competition, and changes in federal and state policy. At the same time, this study found that the management decisions which shaped a college's academic, physical, and social climate significantly impacted its ability to attract students and respond effectively to declining conditions. Specific strategies facilitating recovery from enrollment decline included: 1) attracting new revenue sources; 2) improving retention; 3) improving the quality of student life and campus climate; 4) tightening academic standards and attracting brighter students, and 5) achieving an optimal academic program mix. Mingle and Norris conclude with a six-point prescription for colleges facing decline: 1) no single strategy should be relied upon; 2) a combination of program

A campus ethos which promoted a sense of care and concern for the individual seemed to have a positive impact on enrollment.

terminations, staffing adjustments, administrative consolidation, and cutbacks in course offerings should be considered; 3) strong leadership is a critical component to a successful response; 4) boldness in action is essential; 5) incrementalism does not work under conditions of decline, and 6) successful retrenchments cut deeply enough to meet the immediate and projected shortfalls but not so deep as to prevent the mounting of new revenue-generating efforts.

In a study of small liberal arts colleges which closed their doors during the 1970s, Jonsen (1984) identified the primary reasons influencing institutional demise: 1) there was serious conflict and confusion among internal and external constituents regarding institutional mission and purposes; 2) the financial base was insufficient to support the mission; 3) other elements of financial distress were apparent (e.g., high ratios of student aid expenditures to revenue income, high tuition dependency, and low proportion of total educational and general budget devoted to instructional expenses), and 4) there was a failure in top management, the governing board or both (e.g., governing board tended to be non-involved with college). Jonsen concluded that nearly all of these factors, if recognized in time, were amenable to administrative intervention. Furthermore, he found that the saga of failure for each institution was unique and that, in spite of fiscal and enrollment problems, the external environment rarely acted in isolation in prompting the closing.

In a study conducted to identify the reasons for turnaround in 56 small colleges which had experienced enrollment decline from 1979 to 1983, Parker (1987) found that a strong consensus about mission among institutional constituencies was an asset for reversing a declining enrollment condition. Moreover, she found that absence of consensus or mission confusion was a frequently occurring attribute of stable and declining colleges. While there were no statistically significant differences found on this variable between the improving and stable colleges, Parker concluded that a clearly-defined mission appears to be a stabilizing force and may indeed aid recovery. Likewise, the absence of mission strength may limit recovery or prolong decline. Parker's research suggests that the single most important aspect of recovery from enrollment decline and/or stability is the organization's internal environment. As Parker concludes, "It is perhaps not as much what the organization does but more what it is that predicts the final outcome" (p. 7).

With regard to internal management of decline, Parker and others (Cyert, 1980; Hambrick & Schecter, 1983; Hofer, 1980; Rubin, 1979) have differentiated between strategic and operational responses. Operational responses tend to be efficiency-oriented, to focus on "doing things right," take little time to implement or reverse, require little or no group consensus to implement, and are typically within the control of individual managers (e.g., cutting departmental costs). On the other hand, strategic responses take longer to implement, require at least minimal consensus, typically impact the institution as a whole, represent unusual or radical changes for the organization, and tend to focus on "doing the right things" (e.g. a change in the competitive stance of the institution). Taken together, the research on these two approaches suggests that a strategic approach response may be more important to recovery from decline than additional efficiency measures. In fact, Rubin (1979) found that efficiency may actually be counterproductive for organizations with little or no slack. As noted earlier, Chaffee (1982) argues that successful turnaround requires a combination of efficiency and strategic types of moves. In the study cited above, Parker (1987) found that improving colleges typically employed fewer operating-type responses and more strategic-type responses than declining colleges. Stable colleges employed fewer of either type of response than improving and declining colleges.

A handful of studies have focused exclusively on the response patterns of "successful" colleges. Peck (1984) studied several successful small colleges (each of the colleges met Peck's criteria for success, e.g., sound fiscal condition as measured by positive scores on several financial ratios, modest endowment, FTE less than 2,500, limited geographical drawing area, stable presidential leadership, and college recognized by experts as well-managed) and identified seven characteristics shared by all of these institutions: 1) they were dominated by a commitment to mission and purpose - activities were guided by a strong "strategic vision;" 2) they were opportunity conscious - constantly anticipating changes and identifying opportunities to advance their mission; 3) they were highly innovative and creative; 4) their decisions about the future and change were made largely by intuition - president was actively engaged in "intelligence gathering;" 5) their administrative style was people-oriented versus structural or bureaucratically-oriented; 6) they were effectiveness-oriented more than they were efficiency-oriented, and 7) they were extremely well-run at the operational level.

Peck concluded that the driving force behind the success of these schools was an entrepreneurial leadership style and that effective leadership and effective college management exist in symbiosis. For leadership to be effective, conditions in the college must be receptive to the kind of leadership provided. In

"It is perhaps not as much what the organization does but more what it is that predicts the final outcome" (Parker, 1978).

brief, successful colleges tended to have presidents who focused on building the campus culture through promoting values and a common mission to which the community could eagerly and affirmatively respond. A study yielding similar conclusions was conducted by Hamlin and Hungerford (1988). To determine what measures were used by colleges which had dug themselves out of financial hardship, college presidents were asked to identify tools they found to be of greatest use in overcoming financial insolvency. Two findings were notable: 1) institutions that successfully overcame financial crisis did it by focusing on revenue-enhancing strategies (e.g., expanding recruitment efforts, presidential fundraising efforts, increasing gifts/grants from donors, enhancing presidential public awareness efforts, increasing tuition fees, increasing scholarship funding, and changing/adding programs to meet current market trends/needs) as opposed to decreasing expenses, and 2) the ultimate success or failure in overcoming financial crisis seemed to depend upon the vision, enthusiasm, and business skills of the president. These findings led the authors to conclude that the role of the private college president is undergoing dramatic changes. According to Hamlin and Hungerford, today's successful college president must have stellar communication skills, marketing savvy, and financial acumen in order to lead the institution in a manner that will inspire loyalty and dedication in the face of monumental challenges.

According to St. John (1991), the unexpected resiliency of some private liberal arts colleges during the 1980s can be explained by organizational transformation. In a study of private liberal arts colleges, St. John identified several strategies in use or emphasized at the most successful institutions: 1) honing the academic strategy (e.g., examined and strengthened academic programs, improved faculty, and strengthened mission); 2) improving overall management (e.g., enhancing budgeting and financial planning systems/processes, administrative computing resources, and planning process); 3) implementing enrollment management system with emphasis on recruitment, retention, and financial aid policies and practices; 4) refining pricing strategies (e.g., considering student aid, tuition, and room and board vis-à-vis the competition when setting prices), and 5) pursuing alternative revenue sources (e.g., new off-campus programs, renting out facilities in down times, and partnerships with local business and industry). St. John also found that these schools all had strong presidents who were well versed in contemporary higher education management approaches as well as internal and external constituents exhibiting strong consensus about institutional mission.

Perhaps especially relevant to this research is a study by Hubbard (1985) involving the hallmarks of successful church-related colleges. Based on his review of the literature, Hubbard identifies typical characteristics of thriving church-related colleges: 1) clear identity and distinct educational goals and mission; 2) loyal and vocal alumni; 3) powerful religious commitments; 4) active and involved board of trustees; 5) effective leadership; 6) a "good" story and an effective means for communicating this "story," and 7) intense denominational support.

Summary

The literature reviewed in this chapter falls into three distinct clusters: 1) organizational adaptation; 2) strategic planning and business management, and 3) successful college management. According to the organizational adaptation research, organizations manifesting "self-designing"-type features (i.e., innovation, fluidity, and adaptability) are better equipped to deal with declining conditions than organizations which respond conservatively and rigidly. Specifically, organizations which simultaneously nurture contradictory notions such as adaptability and flexibility, and strong mission and vigorous change and movement, are able to cope better in turbulent and unpredictable times. From the strategic planning and business management literature, we learn that an "interpretive" strategy may ultimately be more useful for achieving resiliency. Perhaps the most striking finding from the successful college management literature involves the consensus about the kinds of characteristics found in the most resilient institutions: strong commitment to mission and purposes, an innovative and creative ethos, an opportunity-conscious orientation, an effectiveness-driven stance, a revenue-generating focus, and exceptional presidential leadership.

While the above research covers a wide range of methodological and disciplinary perspectives, three common themes are evident. First, both internal and external factors play a role in influencing institutional performance. Second, managers can act to successfully influence institutional outcomes. Third, the evidence is clear that when facing decline, avoiding the understandable tendency to hunker down and respond conservatively is important. As will be demonstrated in the next chapter, the experiences of the most resilient Christian liberal arts colleges and universities provide even more striking support for these notions.

CHAPTER FOUR
The Characteristics of Resilient Christian Colleges and Universities

The Characteristics of Resilient Christian Colleges and Universities

"There are things that even a beleaguered college can do that will enable it to survive and increase its value" (Scarlett, 1982).

Almost no one could have fully predicted the stormy changes in recent years that have characterized the environment in which colleges and universities are situated. Yet, in spite of challenges that might appear insurmountable, a number of institutions have survived — and thrived. The successful adaptation of the Christian liberal arts college and university is a particularly interesting phenomenon. As noted in the previous chapter, this sector, on average, far outpaced national private college undergraduate enrollment norms during the 1980s.

Given the adversity facing all of higher education, how does one account for the resiliency of Christian colleges and universities, a sector fitting well the type of institution predicted by many doomsayers to be at high risk to the stressful conditions of the 1980s and 1990s? What factors might account for the strengthened position which many of these institutions are enjoying? Most importantly, what did the leaders of the most resilient of these institutions do to facilitate their institutions' success? This chapter answers these questions by overviewing the characteristics which distinguish the most resilient Christian colleges and universities from the other institutions in the study.

The findings of the study reveal that the more resilient institutions can be distinguished from the other institutions on several key variables, including inherent institutional characteristics as well as specific management strategies. Happily, the findings suggest that the resiliency of the most successful of these institutions is attributable, at least in part, to specific actions which were taken and strategies which were implemented by institutional leaders. The most significant of these characteristics are reviewed and discussed in the following sections.

Inherent Institutional Characteristics

As noted in the previous chapter, there is some debate among researchers regarding the extent to which resiliency can be influenced by managerial actions versus external forces or inherent organizational characteristics which are beyond the control of institutional leaders. The results of this study suggest that the resiliency of the Christian colleges and universities is due to a combination of managerial influence and environmental factors, as well as unique organizational features. Pertaining to the latter, three characteristics are significant: 1) environmental setting and location; 2) breadth of undergraduate student drawing area, and 3) the extent to which the campus is residential in nature.

Findings suggest that both geographical location and environmental setting may have contributed in some part to the changing conditions of the Christian colleges and universities. For example, as described in Chapter Two, Declining institutions are much more likely to be found in regions which experienced sharper drops in the number of high school graduates during the 1980s (59% of the Declining schools are located in the Northcentral and Northeastern regions of the country versus 44% of the Stable and 39% of the Improving institutions). Especially for those institutions focused primarily on the traditional-aged undergraduate population and drawing their students from a regional market base, such an influence is perhaps not surprising.

Likewise, a higher percentage of the Declining institutions are located in urban settings than small towns or rural communities (59% of the Declining schools are located in very large cities or towns versus 46% of Stable and 39% of Improving institutions). As noted in Chapter Two, this finding contradicts research which cites the urban setting as an advantage for overcoming conditions of scarcity (see, for example, Tempel, 1985). Given the market base from which many of the Coalition schools draw students (i.e., religiously conservative church backgrounds), it might be that the urban Christian college or university is a less desirable option for the "typical" evangelical Christian college-goer than the institution located in a more sheltered and pristine setting. Some support for this notion can be found in the works of modern-day prophets such as John Perkins (1993), Tony Campolo (1994), and Ray Bakke (1987), who suggest that the contemporary evangelical community has increasingly disengaged itself from the urban center.

A second finding which contradicts previous research involves the breadth of an institution's undergraduate student drawing area. Since 1981, the Improving institutions have enrolled a significantly higher percentage of in-state students than either the Stable or Declining institutions (63% versus 55% and 50%, respectively). Moreover, the regression analysis using the index as the independent variable (see Table 25) found that of all the dependent variables, the percentage of in-state students made the greatest contribution to positive change in institutional condition. As discussed in Chapter Three, several studies have found that a national student recruitment base contributes to increased enrollment stability, particularly during turbulent times. However, Buffington's 1990 study which used a population comparable to the one used for this study (moderately-selective four-year liberal arts colleges), also found a positive relationship between enrollment growth and the percentage of in-state students enrolled on the campus. It could be that for such institutions, greater dependence upon a local or regional market helps to buffer the institution from national enrollment fluctuations or economic trends.

Table 25. **Significant Forced Entry Regression Results of Weighted Index on the Selected Independent Variables**

Independent Variable	Beta Weight	P =
Proportion of in-state students	0.5404	0.0068
Proportion of commuting students	-0.4733	0.0157

$R2 = .3724$
Adjusted $R2 = .3126$
$DF = 2,21$

> The results of this study suggest that the resiliency of the Christian colleges and universities is due to a combination of managerial influence and environmental factors, as well as unique organizational features.

The third and final institutional characteristic worth noting involves the campus environment, particularly as related to the extent to which the undergraduate student population is residential versus commuting in nature. While the Coalition schools have a significantly higher residential student population than national norms for all private four-year colleges (80% versus 69%), the Improving and Stable institutions boast a slightly greater residential population in 1991 (81% and 82%, respectively, versus 78% for the Declining schools). Moreover, the Improving schools made the greatest gains during the 1980s in increasing their residential population (from 73% in 1981 to 81% in 1991). In addition, as Table 25 shows, the percent of commuting students negatively impacts institutional condition; in other words, as the share of commuting students on the campus increases, overall institutional condition appears to weaken. A growing residential student population carries with it several side benefits which might potentially influence an institution's overall condition with perhaps the most significant being the increased revenue which comes from room and board fees, as well as increased student involvement leading to enhanced student satisfaction, morale, and retention.

Patterns in Strategy Usage

The analyses conducted on the data yielded significant distinctions with regard to the frequency and nature of strategies employed during the 1980s by colleges with differing conditions. While a number of items were statistically significant at the .05 level or less, the difference in the pattern of strategy usage between the Improving, Stable, and Declining institutions is striking. What is most relevant here are the differences between the Improving institutions and others. In examining the pattern of strategies employed by the Improving schools, eight characteristics emerge. These characteristics are:

1. The Improving schools exhibit the highest level and broadest range of activity during the 1980s;
2. The Improving schools exhibit a slightly stronger commitment to mission and purpose;
3. The Improving schools are more likely to reflect *Janusian* thinking characteristics;
4. The Improving schools are more concerned about effectiveness than efficiency;
5. The Improving schools exhibit a more caring campus culture;
6. The Improving schools are more focused on strengthening their images and their relationships with important external constituencies;
7. The Improving schools employ "interpretive" strategies more consistently and to a greater extent than do Stable or Declining institutions, and
8. The Improving schools are more likely to be perceived as being led by highly effective presidents.

Highest level and broadest range of activity

Of the three groups of institutions, the Improving schools exhibit the highest level of activity during the 1980s and are engaged in launching simultaneously a wide variety of strategies. For example, of the 220 survey items, the Improving schools report having employed 60% of the strategies to a moderate extent or greater during the 1980s while the Stable and Declining schools report having employed 51% and 43% of the strategies. Perhaps even more significantly, the Improving institutions did not hunker down and focus on a narrowly prescribed range of strategies. Instead, they pursued a wide ranging and diverse course of action such as the following:

- Strengthening their traditional undergraduate programs while adding graduate programs and expanding course offerings for non-traditional adult students;
- Expanding recruitment efforts simultaneously with traditional-aged undergraduates, part-time students, international students, and students from the sponsoring denomination;

- Adding new programs to attract academically strong students while strengthening support services for academically weaker students, and
- Strengthening revenue-generating efforts (fundraising, recruitment, and new program development initiatives) while undertaking cost-containment measures.

Why is the range of strategy important? For many of the Improving institutions, the leveraging of a broad range of initiatives increased the chances that something would go right while decreasing the risks associated with putting all of ones' eggs in one basket. To quote one president, "Had we played it safe and focused only on our traditional undergraduate programs and markets during the 1980s, I have no doubt that our institution would be in much worse shape in the 1990s. Instead, the success of some of the new ventures that we implemented a decade ago — like our programs for returning adults — gave us a safety net which, subsequently, helped us better weather the ups and downs...and nothing breeds success like success."

When all is said and done, the resiliency of the Improving institutions cannot be attributed to any single strategy or institutional characteristic. What does seem to be very important is the overall level and breadth of activity that is sustained over time. For each of the Improving institutions, the mix of strategy is slightly different. However, the one thing that is common across all 28 schools is that a high enough level of activity was maintained so that a sense of synergy developed; something in that synergy took hold and provided the necessary impetus for achieving higher levels of effectiveness. One respondent described this well when he wrote about how the addition of graduate programs at his institution provided the unexpected bonus of increased visibility for the undergraduate programs and subsequent enrollment growth on both levels.

Another respondent wrote about the difficulty of quantifying precisely the formula for success: "The exact reason for our success over the past several years is really something of a mystery. Quite frankly, I think that our success is due to doing enough of the right things, having enough of these right things work, and having a little luck along the way. To pin our success on any single strategy is probably a mistake. Somewhere in the combination of the things we have done is the key to our success — but it is beyond me to tell you exactly how it worked!"

Commitment to mission and purposes

As Table 26 shows, the Improving schools exhibit a slightly stronger commitment to mission and purposes than the Stable or Declining institutions. They are more likely to be engaged in strategic

> *When all is said and done, the resiliency of the Improving institutions cannot be attributed to any single strategy or institutional characteristic.*

planning efforts, to have recently revised their mission and to refer to their mission in everyday decision making and program development. In general, these schools seem to have a strong, collective sense about who they are, where they are going, and why they exist and they use this knowledge in very intentional ways.

Table 26. **Items Reflecting Commitment to Mission and Purpose**

	\multicolumn{6}{c}{*Means and Standard Deviations by Group*}
	\multicolumn{2}{c}{Improving}	\multicolumn{2}{c}{Stable}	\multicolumn{2}{c}{Declining}
	Mean	S.D.	Mean	S.D.	Mean	S.D.
College operates with liberal arts mission	4.52	0.589	4.33	0.686	4.27	0.631
There is a general sense that this college has a distinctive purpose to fulfill	4.21	0.645	4.05	0.725	4.13	0.639
Mission statement is referred to in decision-making	4.21	0.816	4.05	0.639	3.95	0.785
There is an effective means of conveying our mission to our publics	3.81	0.912	3.61	0.777	3.51	0.811
This college has a special identity, unlike any other in higher education	3.52	1.011	3.17	1.151	3.36	1.011
The mission statement has been revised	3.40	1.441	2.38	1.241	3.18	1.331
Developed and implemented strategic plan	3.92	0.954	3.66	0.971	3.51	1.263
Trustees are generally supportive of the mission	4.76	0.435	4.55	0.615	4.59	0.591
Our academic programs clearly reflect our mission	4.42	0.504	4.33	0.485	4.36	0.581

Rating scale: 1 = not at all   3 = to some extent   5 = to a great extent

Having clarity and strength of mission may contribute to institutional resiliency in at least two key ways: 1) A strong sense of mission, when effectively communicated, can be exciting and motivating for internal as well as external constituencies. People are undoubtedly more willing to follow (and to put their support behind) an institution that has a clear and compelling story to tell. 2) The most effective and powerful leveraging of resources is typically undergirded by a clear understanding of institutional strengths, weaknesses, potential, and liabilities. Especially when resources are limited, it is essential that resources be invested to support those efforts which will yield the greatest return. A strong mission provides a powerful mechanism for prioritizing and allocating scarce resources. Not surprising, then, is research which finds that the absence of strong mission may actually limit recovery from adversity or prolong organizational decline (see, for example, Parker, 1987). As Peter Drucker (1980) puts it, "The failure to give adequate thought to business purpose and mission is perhaps the most important single cause of business frustration and business failure" (p. 127).

Janusian thinking characteristics

> The Improving institutions are engaged in ventures which suggest a spirit of innovation and entrepreneurship.

In today's unstable, unpredictable, and increasingly competitive environment, it is perhaps not surprising that the most resilient institutions are more proactive, exhibiting a greater degree of creativity and adaptability than the other schools. Indeed, as Table 27 shows, the Improving institutions are engaged in ventures which suggest a spirit of innovation and entrepreneurship, and survey responses confirm a flexible and responsive ethos on their campuses. Several authors (Cameron, 1984; Cyert, 1980; Hedberg, Nystrom, & Starbuck, 1976) have argued that even while a proactive management stance may feel counterintuitive to leaders (when facing fiscal stress, the natural tendency is to become self-protective, conservative, and rigid), an opportunistic approach is essential when facing stressful conditions.

What is important here is that the Improving institutions are not pursuing this approach in isolation. With one eye focused squarely on the horizon in search of new opportunities, the Improving schools are at the same time honing their missions and strengthening their identities. When all is said and done, the resiliency of these institutions may be due in large part to their ability to successfully balance these two opposing forces — in short, to practice *Janusian* thinking. Indeed, as Cameron found in his research (see Chapter Three), the interplay between actions which simultaneously nurture both stability and adaptability may be one of the most important findings of this study. It is as if these elements empower, augment, and bolster each other: the strong mission provides a coherent foundation and a secure identity around which the institution can evolve, innovate, and change, while the push to move forward establishes a culture committed to the positive, indeed necessary evolution, innovation, and change to assure the institution's ongoing competitiveness and viability.

Effectiveness versus efficiency

The strategies employed by the Improving colleges and universities suggest that these schools are adopting to various extent the approach touted by leaders of the contemporary Total Quality Management (TQM) movement. As Table 28 illustrates, these institutions are seeking to improve the quality of their operations,

Table 27. **Items Reflecting Opportunistic Stance**

	Means and Standard Deviations by Group					
	Improving		Stable		Declining	
	Mean	S.D.	Mean	S.D.	Mean	S.D.
Constructed or bought additional physical plant	3.88	1.054	3.35	1.222	3.19	1.289
Added graduate-level programs and courses	2.54	1.141	2.44	1.338	1.91	1.019
Spirit of entrepreneurship is encouraged: innovative ideas are rewarded	3.52	1.046	3.11	0.832	3.27	0.767
Expanded student early enrollment options	2.73	1.287	2.33	0.971	2.13	0.941
Developed new on-campus programs to serve new markets	3.41	0.775	3.17	1.098	3.31	1.171
Initiated truly innovative programs and courses	2.79	1.021	2.61	0.851	2.63	1.049
Innovative activity is increasing	3.44	0.768	3.11	0.832	3.41	0.734
Expanded recruitment efforts	4.44	0.712	4.11	0.676	4.22	0.685
Established new domains of activity	3.41	1.041	2.78	0.943	2.81	0.795
Expanded recruitment of part-time students	4.08	0.901	3.61	1.145	3.68	1.323
We tend to do more of what we do well; to expand in our areas of expertise	3.61	0.764	3.33	0.841	3.36	0.789
Expanded recruitment of adult students	3.21	1.371	2.66	1.455	3.04	1.397
Added adult degree completion program	3.33	1.494	2.83	1.723	3.01	1.512
Expanded recruitment of international students	2.91	1.041	2.83	0.923	2.86	1.125
Expanded course offering days/times	2.91	1.101	2.51	0.985	2.22	1.192
Changed curriculum in response to market demands	3.51	0.834	3.11	0.583	3.18	0.733

Rating scale: 1 = not at all   3 = to some extent   5 = to a great extent

including both people and programs. Indeed, the Improving institutions appear able and willing to undertake even the most difficult of tasks (such as releasing less competent staff) for the purpose of making things better. In general, they appear to be more concerned about "doing the right things" than "doing things right." As the research cited in the previous chapter makes clear, the ability to break through the cycle of decline requires the constant nurturing of innovation and the flow of new ideas; the willingness continually to ask and seek answers to the question, "How can we be better today than we were yesterday?" Many side benefits accrue from an effectiveness orientation: students are likely to feel that their needs are being attended to, faculty and staff morale may be increased, and the confidence of important constituents is likely to be heightened.

Table 28. **Items Reflecting Effectiveness Orientation**

	\multicolumn{6}{c}{Means and Standard Deviations by Group}
	Improving		Stable		Declining	
	Mean	S.D.	Mean	S.D.	Mean	S.D.
Our campus is concerned with providing students with a high quality educational experience	4.71	0.464	4.51	0.857	4.51	0.597
Faculty are involved in ongoing program review/revision	3.95	0.806	3.67	1.029	3.91	0.898
Those making a personal and/or financial investment in our college feel that they receive an ample return	3.96	0.675	3.77	0.428	3.77	0.612
Trustees are primarily involved in broad policy issues	4.16	0.554	3.51	0.857	3.99	0.873
Increased the emphasis on strategic planning	3.81	1.001	3.27	1.178	3.63	1.048
Increased the quality of our senior administrators	3.52	0.872	3.27	1.137	3.36	1.144
Our senior administrators have high credibility	3.84	0.688	3.72	1.071	3.63	0.789
Our trustees have high credibility	3.56	0.821	3.27	0.669	3.54	0.911

Rating scale: 1 = not at all   3 = to some extent   5 = to a great extent

In contrast, as Table 29 shows, the Declining institutions in the study are following an approach which might be characterized as cautious, efficient and conservative. These schools tend to be focused primarily on preserving resources and on cutting back programs and decreasing and/or deferring spending. Given the difficult circumstances in which many of the Declining institutions find themselves at the end of the 1980s, such an approach is understandable. However, the reader needs to keep in mind that at the beginning and even into the mid-1980s, the majority of these schools were in fairly good condition. Indeed, the conditions of the Improving and Declining schools are, on average, reversed from what they were in 1981. To what extent the more conservative management approach facilitated the spiral of decline is a difficult thing to discern. What is safe to assume is this: an exclusive focus on cutting back and preserving resources without a concurrent growth strategy, may, and probably will, over time leave a campus demoralized and further weaken efforts to garner students or financial support.

Table 29. Items Reflecting Conservatism and Resource Preservation Stance

	Declining Mean	Declining S.D.	Stable Mean	Stable S.D.	Improving Mean	Improving S.D.
Improved budgeting and cost-control systems	3.68	1.152	3.05	0.857	3.48	1.091
Deferred maintenance and repair funding	3.01	1.225	2.82	1.15	2.72	1.208
Decreased equipment funding	2.95	1.112	2.58	1.223	2.44	1.083
Reduced non-academic programs through selective cuts	2.52	0.681	2.05	0.899	1.96	0.676
Used part-time faculty in administrative positions	2.09	0.845	1.94	0.857	1.95	0.971
Froze faculty and staff salaries	2.01	1.095	1.64	0.931	1.84	1.344
Increased faculty to student ratio	2.09	0.868	1.51	0.514	1.83	0.816
Reduced academic programs through selective cuts	2.67	0.483	2.01	0.791	1.81	0.764
Eliminated unprofitable academic programs	2.14	0.964	1.82	0.636	1.76	0.879
Eliminated unprofitable co-curricular programs	2.33	1.016	1.64	0.702	1.81	1.001
Merged departments and programs	2.09	0.768	1.76	0.562	1.56	0.768
Negotiated early retirement with senior staff/faculty	2.14	0.911	1.53	0.624	1.52	0.963
Dismissed non-tenured faculty in low demand areas	1.85	0.793	1.52	0.717	1.44	0.583
Eliminated professional staff positions	2.14	0.793	1.71	0.772	1.36	0.491
Increased faculty teaching loads	1.41	0.591	1.22	0.732	1.33	0.637
Reduced faculty size through natural attrition	2.01	0.894	1.58	0.618	1.32	0.627
Reduced professional staff size through natural attrition	1.95	0.865	1.52	0.624	1.32	0.557
Cut back athletic programs	1.68	1.041	1.11	0.323	1.28	0.614
Reduced co-curricular programs through across-the-board cuts	2.01	0.949	1.52	0.701	1.24	0.436
Reduced academic programs through across-the-board cuts	1.71	0.845	1.35	0.606	1.21	0.408
Reduced faculty and staff salaries	1.33	1.143	1.01	0.001	1.08	0.277
Dismissed tenured faculty in low demand areas	1.23	0.625	1.17	0.529	1.08	0.277
Reallocated funds from low demand areas to high demand areas	3.01	0.816	2.67	0.841	2.54	0.779
Used gift money to reduce reliance on tuition income	2.95	1.161	2.64	1.115	2.44	1.003

Rating scale: 1 = not at all   3 = to some extent   5 = to a great extent

Survival Strategies for Christian Colleges and Universities

An exclusive focus on cutting back and preserving resources without a concurrent growth strategy, may, and probably will, over time leave a campus demoralized and further weaken efforts to garner students or financial support.

A caring campus culture

A related point involves the considerable attention that the Improving schools are giving to enhancing the campus experience for internal constituencies. For example, as Table 30 shows, they are improving the communication and information flow, thus enabling campus participants to feel more involved in and informed about college processes and events. Research has shown that during times of flux, consistent, direct communication between the administration and staff and faculty is essential for reducing the uncertainty, negative thinking, and rumor-mongering which frequently accompanies such times (Galbraith, 1977).

The Improving institutions are also making numerous changes to improve the quality of the student experience, including such areas as academic advising, academic support, new student orientation and registration, and career planning.

Table 30. Items Reflecting Caring Campus Culture

| | \multicolumn{6}{c}{Means and Standard Deviations by Group} |
| | Improving | | Stable | | Declining | |
	Mean	S.D.	Mean	S.D.	Mean	S.D.
Improved religious life programs	3.75	0.794	3.16	0.785	3.41	0.854
Improved student development	3.58	0.511	3.16	0.711	3.31	0.779
Added summer advising/ registration for new students	3.51	0.121	3.44	0.124	3.31	0.991
Strengthened academic support services	3.51	0.831	2.94	0.111	3.05	0.781
Improved academic advising services	3.25	0.741	3.22	0.941	2.81	0.731
Improved career planning services	3.25	0.851	3.39	0.921	2.63	0.851
Added summer orientation program	3.01	1.251	2.77	1.431	2.31	1.281
This campus is concerned with providing students with a high quality experience	4.71	0.464	4.51	0.857	4.51	0.597
The senior administration demonstrates concern for the welfare of students and each other	4.51	0.589	4.38	0.697	4.22	0.751
This college places emphasis on serving students	4.37	0.646	4.33	0.686	4.36	0.789
Made changes to improve the campus climate	3.71	0.551	3.44	0.855	3.54	0.857
Improved campus information systems	3.64	0.811	3.11	1.021	3.51	0.859
Enhanced faculty development programs	3.17	0.916	3.11	0.963	3.01	1.191
Conflict is not increasing within our institution	4.48	0.714	4.39	0.916	4.27	0.935
When they occur, cutbacks are implemented on a prioritized basis	3.54	1.141	3.26	0.883	3.42	0.811

Rating scale: 1 = not at all   3 = to some extent   5 = to a great extent

In general, these institutions exhibit a strong commitment to meeting the needs of their students. It makes sense that the nurturing of a campus climate wherein faculty, staff, and students feel comfortable, supported, and valued might positively impact institutional success. Faculty and staff who feel good about their role in the institution are apt to carry these feelings of good will over into their interactions with students. And, the existence on the campus of a strong support network, designed to facilitate student growth and success, makes an obvious statement to students regarding their value to the institution. Indeed, a number of researchers (Bean, 1983; Crockett, 1985; Levitz & Noel, 1995) have noted the importance of strong academic advising and career planning programs to student success and retention on the campus. Contemporary business literature suggests that "the effective organization stays close to its customers" (Peters & Waterman, 1982). The same adage may be true for colleges and universities: successful institutions know their students, anticipate their needs and wants, and are committed to meeting these needs to the greatest extent possible.

Focus on image

The focus of the Improving institutions is not only internal; these schools also appear to be very concerned about strengthening their effectiveness vis-à-vis their external publics. As noted in the Chapter Two, the Improving schools report the greatest progress in strengthening academic standards (e.g., ACT/SAT scores, high school preparation, general selectivity) and also show the most significant progress in raising admissions standards (e.g., declining acceptance rates coupled with increasing matriculation rates). Such findings confirm previously conducted research which hinted at a possible link between efforts to strengthen academic reputation and enrollment growth (Breneman, 1983; Mingle & Norris, 1981).

As Table 31 shows, the Improving schools are also making a concerted effort to strengthen their relationships with important external constituencies, including sponsoring denominations, the community, and business and industry, as well as bolstering institutional public relations and fundraising efforts. In general, these institutions appear to be making concerted efforts to refine and improve the way in which they are viewed by important constituencies, as well as to use the knowledge that they have about themselves to intentionally shape the messages which are communicated to these same bodies. In a world where the boundaries between organizations and their external environments are increasingly fluid, and where organizations are increasingly dependent upon such environments to sustain an adequate flow of resources (be they students, financial, or other), it is not surprising that activities which bolster the institution's credibility and legitimacy in the eyes of its stakeholders might also contribute to its resiliency.

Table 31. **Items Reflecting Image Cultivation Efforts**

| | **Means and Standard Deviations by Group** | | | | | |
| | *Improving* | | *Stable* | | *Declining* | |
	Mean	S.D.	Mean	S.D.	Mean	S.D.
Strengthened relations with sponsoring church	3.32	1.181	2.83	1.211	3.13	1.281
Increased the president's public relations efforts	4.16	0.851	3.83	1.043	3.72	1.032
Strengthened community support	3.32	0.901	2.88	0.901	3.27	0.827
Strengthened the public relations effort	3.68	0.627	3.33	0.767	3.59	0.854
Increased fundraising efforts with trustees	4.01	0.866	3.64	0.862	3.66	1.111
Increased fundraising efforts with alumni	3.96	0.735	3.82	0.636	3.71	0.902
Increased fundraising efforts with private foundations	3.56	1.193	3.17	1.185	3.28	1.007
Increased fundraising efforts with business/industry	3.44	1.121	3.05	1.144	3.38	0.973
College leaders make a concerted effort to educate important stakeholders about the college's value	3.68	0.945	3.17	0.786	3.59	0.959
Expanded recruitment of students from sponsoring church	4.08	0.901	3.61	1.145	3.68	1.323
Added special programs to attract high-ability students	3.17	1.114	2.95	1.111	2.54	1.184

Rating scale: 1 = not at all   3 = to some extent   5 = to a great extent

Use of "interpretive" strategy

As defined by Chaffee (see Chapter Three), adaptive strategists are concerned with aligning the organization with the environment; for example, they advocate changing the organizational orientation to meet current demands and thus ensure the continued flow of resources. Interpretive strategists, on the other hand, are concerned with how organizational participants see, understand, and feel about their lives within the organization. With the latter approach, effective action involves shaping the values, symbols, and emotions that influence the behaviors of individuals. Consistent with Chaffee's findings, the Improving schools are employing a healthy mix of adaptive and interpretive strategy with slightly more emphasis on the latter. As shown in Table 32, the interpretive strategies receiving the most emphasis by these institutions include those aimed at strengthening mission, improving the functioning of trustees, and enhancing image or external orientation.

As Chaffee suggests, it could be that while both approaches facilitate growth and well-being, it is the extent to which the interpretive strategy is employed that determines the ultimate degree of resiliency attained. Given the world in which Christian colleges and universities are situated (with their narrowly focused mission and resource base), it makes sense that strategies which emanate from the institution's essential character and self-identity, which resonate with the values and beliefs held by important stakeholders, and which cultivate credibility and legitimacy might also enhance resiliency. Particularly during turbulent times, the survival of such institutions undoubtedly rests upon the support of loyal constituencies who fully believe in the institutional story and who are willing to go to great lengths to ensure the endurance of that story.

Effective presidents

In the survey's open-ended section in which respondents are asked to indicate reasons for changes in institutional condition during the 1980s, more than half of the Improving institutions attribute their bettering conditions to the quality of presidential leadership. For example, consider the following response, typical of many received from Improving institutions: "Our turnaround began with the inauguration of _____ _____ as president. His energy, vision, and knowledge about what needed to be done coupled with his willingness to take risks and innovate moved our school from a very dismal place in 1981 to an exciting time in the 1990s. There is a great deal of excitement on the campus now about where we are headed!" Survey respondents frequently use words like "visionary," "risk-taker,""change agent," "people-oriented," "entrepreneurial," and "good communicator" to describe the leaders who oversaw their institutions during the 1980s.

Chaffee's research found that the greater resiliency of the successful colleges in her study could be attributed in large part to presidents with excellent communication skills. (Good communication skills are obviously essential for the carrying out of most of the other characteristics described above.) According to Chaffee, these presidents were especially effective at focusing and articulating the missions of the colleges they led. In particular, they were able to mirror back to important constituencies both overt and obscure institutional values and beliefs. In doing so, presidents helped campus participants develop a greater sense of meaning for their individual roles and activities, thereby creating a unified vision and sense of purpose across

Successful institutions know their students, anticipate their needs and wants, and are committed to meeting these needs to the greatest extent possible.

Table 32. **Comparison of Adaptive and Interpretive Strategy Usage for Improving, Stable and Declining Colleges**

	\multicolumn{6}{c}{Means and Standard Deviations by Group}
	Improving		Stable		Declining	
	Mean	S.D.	Mean	S.D.	Mean	S.D.
Adaptive Strategy:						
Attract	3.15	0.417	3.09	0.351	3.13	0.312
Produce	3.12	0.474	3.01	0.529	2.85	0.521
Research	2.73	0.481	2.61	0.419	3.06	0.423
Change	2.59	0.326	2.55	0.395	2.78	0.425
Conserve	1.91	0.258	1.87	0.304	2.22	0.291
Interpretive Strategy:						
Mission	3.91	0.394	3.74	0.344	3.78	0.397
Cooperate	3.77	0.297	3.76	0.345	3.79	0.401
Trustees	3.73	0.387	3.53	0.394	3.68	0.427
Image	3.29	0.389	3.12	0.342	3.25	0.441
Program Focus	2.34	0.381	2.38	0.358	2.38	0.323

Rating scale: 1 = not at all   3 = to some extent   5 = to a great extent

Key for Variables:
Attract = Changes made to attract or retain students
Produce = Changes made in products or services
Research = Research and planning strategies
Change = Strategies reflecting increased receptiveness to change
Conserve = Strategies reflecting resource-conservation efforts
Mission = Strategies to strengthen mission or reflecting strong mission
Cooperate = Strategies to strengthen communication or reflecting good communication and cooperation between campus factions
Trustees = Strategies to strengthen or better involve trustees
Image = Strategies to strengthen image and cultivate external networks
Program Focus = Strategies reflecting academic program refinement

the campus. The findings of this study suggest that a similar force is at work in the more resilient Coalition institutions. As one respondent commented: "Our president has a keen sense about who we are and who we might best serve educationally. The programs implemented over the past several years under his leadership have been right on target and have moved us ahead in ways that none of us dreamed possible. He helped the entire campus, from the Board of Trustees to the faculty to the students, feel good about itself again."

Summary

The findings highlighted in this chapter suggest a number of possible explanations for why some Coalition schools have achieved greater levels of resiliency than others over the past decade. The Improving institutions are differentiated from the Stable and Declining schools both by inherent institutional characteristics and by the strategies that they have implemented. Regarding the former, the Improving schools were more likely to be located in rural or suburban communities, suggesting that an urban location is potentially disadvantageous for the Christian college or university. These schools were also more likely to enroll a significantly higher percentage of in-state students, suggesting that Christian colleges and universities may be helped by expanding markets close to home.

Happily, the results suggest that there are things that leaders can do to influence the condition of their institutions. For example, the Improving institutions were more likely to have strengthened academic standards, expanded their residential population, added new markets, and increased enrollments on all levels and across a wide range of markets. In general, these schools exhibited a stronger commitment to mission, made greater strides in enhancing the overall campus climate including the quality of student life, and adopted an opportunistic mode of operation. One obvious factor is that the Improving institutions engaged in a greater number of programs and strategies, and did so more frequently, than the Stable or Declining schools. Perhaps more important than the use of any specific strategy is the mix of strategies employed, the general level of overall activity sustained, and the unique cultural context within which the strategies are employed.

Happily, the results suggest that there are things that leaders can do to influence the condition of their institutions.

CHAPTER FIVE

Lessons for Institutional Leaders

Lessons for Institutional Leaders

Christian colleges and universities that have prospered where others have failed over the last decade have done so not by hunkering down and waiting for better days. Instead, these schools have established cultures committed to the positive, indeed necessary evolution, innovation, and change to assure their ongoing competitiveness and viability.

The literature reviewed in Chapter Three and the experiences of the 81 Coalition institutions suggest that, when all is said and done, there is no finite prescription for resiliency. The experience of each of the 28 Improving institutions examined in this study is unique, impacted by a mélange of intervening factors. Perhaps more important than the use of any specific strategy or the role of any particular characteristic is the overall approach and the peculiar mix of factors in play at those schools achieving resiliency. While the following list of recommendations for institutional response attempts to capture the most important elements of this mix, the reader is cautioned that any institutional action must be contextualized to fit the unique environment in which the college or university resides.

With this in mind, the findings reported in Chapter Four have led to the development of seven recommendations for institutional leaders to consider:

1. *Pursue a diverse and broad mix of strategies.*

A review of the literature and the experience of the 81 colleges in this study reveal that the factors affecting institutional resiliency and/or decline are complex. More important than the specific strategies employed by an institution is the overall mix of strategies, the general level of activity, and the cultural context within which the management approach is implemented. The Improving colleges in this study exhibited the highest level of activity over the past decade and were engaged in launching a wide variety of efforts simultaneously. By pursuing a wide range of strategy, colleges improve their chances that something will go right while reducing the potential impact of failed ventures. Moreover, there appears to be a synergistic force at work in the resiliency of the Improving colleges. In the deployment of a combination of diverse strategies, something took hold and catapulted these schools to higher levels of effectiveness. The force may not be a predictable one. Indeed, the specific strategy employed is probably not as important as the overall level of activity maintained and the unique mix of strategy employed.

2. Do everything possible to refine and focus the institution's mission, develop effective and consistent means of communicating the mission to important constituencies, and relate all decision-making and planning efforts — both large and small — to the mission.

Seldom has a truly exceptional institution emerged that was not driven by a distinctive and compelling identity. Indeed, numerous research (see, for example, Clark, 1970; Keller, 1983) points out the importance of a strong, clear mission for marketing and organizational effectiveness. The experience of the Improving colleges in this study further affirms that a clear mission, if convincingly communicated, can enhance institutional effectiveness. Institutions which have a clear understanding of their unique niche in the higher education marketplace are likely to respond effectively and quickly to the changing needs of the marketplace.

Many additional benefits accrue from a strong sense of mission: faculty and staff have a clear sense of where the institution is headed, thus enabling a more secure and motivating work environment; external constituencies may be more willing to support an institution that has a bright and exciting future; and the reference to mission in decision-making allows scarce resources to be used to support efforts which will yield the greatest return. A well-known adage suggests that people give to their dreams. It follows that a strategic challenge for institutional leaders is to articulate dreams worthy of the support of their constituencies. A strong, clear sense of mission makes this challenge somewhat less formidable.

A strategic challenge for institutional leaders is to articulate dreams worthy of the support of their constituencies.

3. In the face of shrinking resources, preserve and highlight sources of opportunity.

During periods of duress and flux, a common tendency for leaders is to become self-protective, rigid, and focused on constraints. For example, when organizational slack is minimal, it is not uncommon for new ideas to be quickly discarded for lack of resources or vision and for "analysis paralysis" to set in. However, the experience of the Improving colleges in this study confirms what much of the recent research on the management of organizational decline suggests: an opportunistic, entrepreneurial management stance is likely to be a more effective orientation during periods of resource scarcity than a conservative, cautious focus.

Indeed, according to the research (Whetten & Cameron, 1985), the most effective administrators do everything possible to improve morale and generate financial support for new ideas. In

An opportunistic, entrepreneurial management stance is likely to be a more effective orientation during periods of resource scarcity than a conservative, cautious focus.

particular, effective administrators convert crises into mandates for improvement; view constraints as challenges to be outwitted; make selective cuts in low priority areas in order to free up funds to support new initiatives; pursue new and/or nontraditional sources of revenue; avoid self-defeating debates over the causes of, and blame for, serious problems; deflect the faculty's attention away from highly visible signs of fiscal distress (e.g., low salaries, larger classes) by generating enthusiasm for new opportunities, and place a high premium on all creative suggestions even when they run counter to conventional wisdom or logic.

4. Realize the impact of external factors and institutional characteristics on efforts to achieve resiliency and respond accordingly.

Many colleges and universities still know far too little about the environment in which they recruit and retain students, generate financial support and other resources. Yet, previous research and the experience of the institutions in this study suggest that enrollment success can be greatly enhanced or hampered by the institutional characteristics of enrolled students (in-state, residential, high academic ability, etc.), by level of selectivity, as well as by external factors like location (region of the country and specific locale).

Institutions should develop a keen understanding of their position in the marketplace, i.e., what distinguishes the institution from its competition, including how their unique context either helps or hurts their efforts to succeed. For example, the typical Christian college or university enrolls, on average, only 7% of all inquiring students and 55% of all accepted applicants. What is known about the 93% of inquiries who do not apply or the 45% of accepted applicants who do not enroll? At minimum, institutions should know something about how they are perceived by both enrolling and non-enrolling students, as well as how these perceptions may differ. They should have a very clear sense about why students choose to enroll or not to enroll at their institution. A very intentional effort should be made to then use this information in the marketing of the institution, to tailor messages regarding the institution's advantages or distinctive features to attract those prospective students who are looking for what the institution has to offer. The successful management of enrollment and development efforts on most college campuses in the 1990s will be built upon this kind of substantial and exhaustive research and information base.

If inquiry reveals that current practices, programs, or institutional characteristics are misaligned with what the market appears to want, institutions should evaluate to what extent they are willing or able to make changes to meet new demands. If institutions are unwilling or unable to alter harmful practices or characteristics (and this may very well be the case for mission reasons), then greater effort must be made in other areas to offset the potentially damaging effects. (For example, if a college decides that its urban location is a major drawback in its recruiting effectiveness but is unable to relocate, marketing efforts should be redirected so as to play up the positive benefits of the urban location.)

5. Practice interpretive leadership.

A review of research and the experience of the Improving colleges in this study corroborate that a leadership approach based on Chaffee's interpretive management strategy is a key variable impacting efforts toward success. In particular, it appears that leaders might be well-advised to base their decisions and actions at least as heavily on symbolic values and events as on substantive ones. As defined by Tierney (1989), symbols exist wherever human activity occurs and can reside in a wide range of message units including acts, events, language, dress, ceremonies, structural roles, and even spatial positions in an organization.

Effective interpretive leaders take the time to get to know the distinct culture of the organizations they lead including such things as environmental characteristics, how decisions get made, how socialization processes happen, how information is used, and what various constituents' expect of leaders (Tierney, 1988). They then use this knowledge to align their own use of symbols with the institution's core cultural values and norms. Not surprisingly, research has shown that groups with strong cultures are most readily influenced by new leaders who are perceived as personifications of, rather than threats to, their shared cultural values (Hollander, 1958). The importance of corroborating one's symbols with the institution's culture is further illustrated by the story about a leader who survived only a short time in his first college presidency. During his first month on the job and eager to symbolize a new and more efficient order of business, this president promptly and with considerable fanfare eliminated the campus weekly afternoon coffee hour. What this leader failed to understand was that this particular campus culture had relied for over 25 years on this time for community building and sustenance and placed significant value on this event.

Effective interpretive leaders also use multiple, and sometimes irrational or impractical symbols, particularly to

Leaders might be well-advised to base their decisions and actions at least as heavily on symbolic values and events as on substantive ones.

communicate important institutional priorities. For example, as Chaffee (1984) tells it, the president of a small, private, liberal arts college during a period of significant decline purchased a neighboring campus in order to diversify the campus geographically and programmatically. Not surprisingly, many campus members were stunned and questioned the wisdom of taking on more debt. What these naysayers failed to see was the symbolic significance of such an act. It served as the focal point for launching an effort to upgrade the institution. A series of new opportunities were ignited from this single decision and enthusiasm was rekindled across the campus. Indeed, this one act became the much needed symbol for transforming the entire institution.

Perhaps most importantly, effective interpretive leaders are closely in tune with how organizational participants see, understand, and feel about their lives within the organization. They carry out tasks by appealing to the human need for meaning, for owning decisions, for positive reinforcement, and for belonging. They err in favor of overcommunication, especially during times of flux, recognizing the need of faculty and staff to be kept informed and to feel influential. In particular, they pay attention to the obvious as well as the obscure messages that are given to campus community members regarding their value to the institution. Any effort or achievement is dependent upon the hard work and commitment of many institutional participants. The extent to which these participants feel motivated and a part of the organizational story could potentially impact the level of achievement ultimately attained.

6. *Respond proactively to meet the needs of students.*

In this study, the Improving colleges made significant efforts to meet the educational and social needs of their prospective and current students. For example, these schools were more likely to have expanded the number of days and times that courses were offered, to have developed new off-campus programs, to have demonstrated increased sensitivity to market demands for "relevant" courses, to have improved student services, religious life programs, advising and registration processes, to have initiated special programs for high ability students, and to have strengthened academic support services. Each of the above items indicates a commitment on the part of these institutions to respond to the needs of the students they wish to attract and retain. Such a commitment can make a powerful statement to students regarding their value as members of the campus community. Indeed, students may be willing to forego the wide range of programs available at the larger, and frequently less expensive public universities if they feel that they are in a place where they belong and where they will be cared for.

7. Nurture the support of key constituencies.

Given the fact that colleges and universities exist in a world where the boundaries between their campuses and the external environments are increasingly fluid, it should not be surprising that the research found that Improving institutions exerted inordinate effort in strengthening relationships with strategic constituencies, as well as in strengthening their image. Unfortunately, the need to continually nurture and court the support of important stakeholders is most commonly overlooked during periods of institutional well-being. Indeed, it is easy to take such support for granted.

A strong, effective, public relations effort is critical for earning and keeping the good will of an institution's publics. As noted in previous chapters, people are more willing to follow and put their support behind institutions that have "good stories" to tell. Leaders are urged to make sure that campus public relations efforts clearly and forcefully support organizational priorities and the telling of that particular institution's story. Communication efforts should be strategic and intentional; all communication vehicles (verbal and written) should consistently communicate the most important messages for each audience. Moreover, communication should be a two-way street: members of key constituencies should be encouraged and given ample opportunity to provide their input on organizational issues. Nothing conveys the sense that you are valued more than when someone asks for and listens to your opinion. Most importantly, leaders should remember that a "good story" bears retelling...and retelling...and retelling. While presidents may tire of "beating a dead horse," followers need and want to be reminded about all of the good that the institution is doing and how their contributions help make this possible.

Even for church-supported colleges and universities, denominational support can no longer be taken for granted. Today's constituents, inside and outside the church, are increasingly sophisticated. Unless a Christian college or university can show that it has as much to offer as its major competitors, students and donors will go elsewhere. Remember Charlie Brown standing on the pitcher's mound lamenting, "How can we lose when we're so sincere?" We *can* lose, if we fail to convincingly make our case... to tell our "good story."

Leaders should remember that a "good story" bears retelling... and retelling... and retelling.

Appendices

Appendix A

List of Participating Member Institutions of the Coalition for Christian Colleges & Universities

- + Anderson University
- + Asbury College
- + Azusa Pacific University
- + Bartlesville Wesleyan College
-     Belhaven College
- + Bethel College (IN)
-     Bethel College (KS)
- + Bethel College (MN)
- + Biola University
-     Bluffton College
- + Bryan College
- + California Baptist College
- + Calvin College
- + Campbellsville College
- + Campbell University
- + Cedarville College
- + Colorado Christian University
-     Cornerstone College
- + Covenant College
- + Dallas Baptist University
- + Dordt College
- + Eastern College
- + Eastern Mennonite University
- + Eastern Nazarene College
-     Erskine College
- + Evangel College
- + Fresno Pacific College
- + Geneva College
- + George Fox College
- + Gordon College
- + Goshen College
-     Grace College
- + Grand Canyon University
- + Greenville College
- + Houghton College
- + Huntington College
- + John Brown University
- + Judson College
- + King College
-     The King's College

+ Lee College
+ LeTourneau University
+ Malone College
+ The Master's College
+ Messiah College
+ Mid-American Nazarene College
   Milligan College
   Mississippi College
   Montreat College
+ Mount Vernon Nazarene College
+ North Park College
+ Northwest Christian College
+ Northwest College
+ Northwestern College (IA)
+ Northwestern College (MN)
+ Northwest Nazarene College
   Nyack College
   Olivet Nazarene University
+ Palm Beach Atlantic
   Point Loma Nazarene College
+ Roberts Wesleyan College
+ Seattle Pacific University
+ Simpson College
+ Southern California College
+ Southern Nazarene University
+ Southern Wesleyan University
+ Spring Arbor College
+ Sterling College
   Tabor College
+ Taylor University
+ Trevecca Nazarene College
+ Trinity Christian College
   Trinity International University
+ Union University
+ University of Sioux Falls
+ Warner Pacific College
+ Warner Southern College
+ Western Baptist College
+ Westmont College
+ Wheaton College
+ Whitworth College

+ Survey Respondent

Survival Strategies for Christian Colleges and Universities

Appendix B

Institutional Code_____

STRATEGIC MANAGEMENT SURVEY

SECTION I: OVERALL INSTITUTIONAL STRATEGY AND PRIORITIES

Please Note: An institutional code has been assigned to each institution and we are asking those who complete different sections of the survey to identify themselves. The code is used in order to match institutional responses with data which are being obtained from other sources as well as to ensure consistency in individual responses across institutions. However, <u>all information will remain confidential. No individual institution's response will be used. Only aggregate figures will be included in the write-up of this research project.</u>

Completed by: _____
Title: _____
Telephone Number: (____)_____ Extension:_____

Responses to this survey are based upon (please check all that apply):
_____ Your personal experience working at this college. Please specify the number of years you have been at this college: _____
_____ Knowledge gained from sources other than your personal experience (i.e., other staff, faculty, historical data/reports, etc.)
_____ Other (please specify: _____)

Please rate your general level of awareness regarding the events which have transpired at your institution during the period 1981-1991: (please circle the appropriate numbers)

No Awareness		Somewhat Aware		Very Aware
1	2	3	4	5

<u>Instructions:</u> The following questions may be answered by filling in a blank or circling the appropriate number to designate your response. Feel free to make comments throughout the survey. There is an open-ended question at the end to provide you an opportunity to express your opinion and to make any additional comments not previously addressed in the survey. This survey should take no longer than 15 minutes to complete.

1. To what extent have the following activities been pursued by your college in the past ten years (1981-1991)?

	Not At All	To A Small Extent	To Some Extent	To A Great Extent	To A Very Great Extent
Expanded recruitment efforts	1	2	3	4	5
Expanded fund-raising efforts of president	1	2	3	4	5
Efforts to increase gifts/grants from benefactors	1	2	3	4	5

	Not At All	To A Small Extent	To Some Extent	To A Great Extent	To A Very Great Extent
Increased public awareness efforts of president	1	2	3	4	5
Changed programs to meet current trends	1	2	3	4	5
Added new academic programs	1	2	3	4	5
Strengthened community financial support	1	2	3	4	5
Strengthened community program support	1	2	3	4	5
Efforts to increase gifts/aid from sponsoring church	1	2	3	4	5
Strengthened relations with sponsoring church	1	2	3	4	5
Creative efforts to meet student needs	1	2	3	4	5
Strengthened athletic programs	1	2	3	4	5
Expanded retention efforts	1	2	3	4	5
Strengthened public relations function	1	2	3	4	5
Strengthened quality and effectiveness of trustees	1	2	3	4	5
Improved campus information systems	1	2	3	4	5
Improved budgeting and cost-control systems	1	2	3	4	5
Organizational restructuring	1	2	3	4	5
Developed and implemented strategic plan	1	2	3	4	5
Hired more competent administrators	1	2	3	4	5
Strengthened the development/ fund-raising function	1	2	3	4	5
Released less competent administrators	1	2	3	4	5
Cut back athletic programs	1	2	3	4	5
Increased emphasis on strategic planning	1	2	3	4	5

2. To what extent are the following statements characteristic of your college in the past ten years (1981-1991)?

	Not At All	To A Small Extent	To Some Extent	To A Great Extent	To A Very Great Extent
The college operates under a liberal arts mission	1	2	3	4	5
The college is appropriately Christian in its character	1	2	3	4	5
The mission statement has been reaffirmed	1	2	3	4	5
The mission statement has been revised	1	2	3	4	5
The mission statement is referred to for guidance in major decision-making	1	2	3	4	5
There is an effective means of conveying the college's mission to the public	1	2	3	4	5
A spirit of entrepreneurship is encouraged and innovative ideas are rewarded	1	2	3	4	5
This college has a special identity, unlike any other in higher education	1	2	3	4	5
There is a general sense that this college has a distinctive purpose to fulfill	1	2	3	4	5
People associated with this college share a common definition of its mission	1	2	3	4	5
Those who make a personal or financial investment in this institution believe that they receive an ample return	1	2	3	4	5

	Not At All	To A Small Extent	To Some Extent	To A Great Extent	To A Very Great Extent
Major decisions are very centralized	1	2	3	4	5
Innovative activity at this college is increasing	1	2	3	4	5
Morale is increasing among members of this institution	1	2	3	4	5
Senior administrators have high credibility	1	2	3	4	5
Conflict is increasing within this institution	1	2	3	4	5
Our senior administrators place emphasis upon educating important outsiders about the value of this college	1	2	3	4	5
This institution tends to do more of what it does well, to expand in areas we have expertise	1	2	3	4	5
This college establishes new domains of activity	1	2	3	4	5
We are increasing the quality of the individuals in top administrative positions	1	2	3	4	5
The trustees are generally supportive of the mission of this college	1	2	3	4	5
Adversarial relations exist between the administration and trustees	1	2	3	4	5

3. To what do you attribute changes in the financial condition of this college during the ten year period 1981-1991?

4. What are the most significant challenges currently facing your college?

Do you wish to receive a copy of the results of this study? Yes _____ No _____

Thank you very much for your assistance.

Institutional Code_____

STRATEGIC MANAGEMENT SURVEY

SECTION II: STUDENT RECRUITMENT AND RETENTION

Please Note: An institutional code has been assigned to each institution and we are asking those who complete different sections of the survey to identify themselves. The code is used in order to match institutional responses with data which are being obtained from other sources as well as to ensure consistency in individual responses across institutions. However, <u>all information will remain confidential. No individual institution's response will be used. Only aggregate figures will be included in the write-up of this research project.</u>

Completed by: _____

Title: _____

Telephone Number: (____)_____ Extension:____

Responses to this survey are based upon (please check all that apply):
_____ Your personal experience working at this college. Please specify the number of years you have been at this college: _____
_____ Knowledge gained from sources other than your personal experience (i.e., other staff, faculty, historical data/reports, etc.)
_____ Other (please specify: _____)

Please rate your general level of awareness regarding the events which have transpired at your institution during the period 1981-1991: (please circle the appropriate numbers)

No Awareness		Somewhat Aware		Very Aware
1	2	3	4	5

<u>Instructions:</u> The following questions may be answered by filling in a blank or circling the appropriate number to designate your response. Feel free to make comments throughout the survey. There is an open-ended question at the end to provide you an opportunity to express your opinion and to make any additional comments not previously addressed in the survey. This survey should take no longer than 15 minutes to complete.

Institutional Characteristics:

1. Which one of the following best characterizes your undergraduate student population?

    1. Primarily local
    2. Primarily within state
    3. Primarily regional
    4. Primarily national

2. Which one of the following statements best describes the general admissions practices of your institution?
   1. Any individual wishing to attend will be admitted without review of conventional academic qualifications.
   2. Any high school graduate (or person with equivalent credentials) will be admitted.
   3. The majority of individuals who meet some specified level of academic achievement or other qualifications above and beyond high school graduation are admitted.
   4. Among those individuals who meet some specified level of academic achievement or other qualifications above and beyond high school graduation, only a limited number will be admitted.

3. Which of the following best describes the enrollment strategy pursued by your college in the 1980's?
   1. Increase enrollments
   2. Maintain enrollments
   3. Reduce enrollments and services

4. Which of the following best describes the enrollment strategy currently being pursued by your college?
   1. Increase enrollments
   2. Maintain enrollments
   3. Reduce enrollments and services
   4. Merge with another college or organization
   5. Change control (become a public institution)

5. How do the admissions standards in place at your institution today compare with those in 1981? (Circle one number on each line)

	Lower	Much Lower	No Change	Higher	Much Higher
1. The general level of selectivity	1	2	3	4	5
2. The level and years of high school course work	1	2	3	4	5
3. High school GPA or rank in class	1	2	3	4	5
4. The level of performance on college admissions tests	1	2	3	4	5

6. What percentage of freshmen in Fall 1991 were accepted as exceptions to formal academic requirements? Enter percentage: _____

7. How does this percentage compare with the percentage of freshmen accepted as exceptions in Fall 1981?
   1. The proportion was lower in 1991 than in 1981.
   2. The proportion was the same.
   3. The proportion was higher in 1991 than in 1981.

8. What percentage of freshmen in Fall 1991 at your institution are taking one or more remedial courses during their first semester or year? Enter percentage: _____

9. How does this percentage compare with the percentage in Fall 1981?
   1. The percentage was smaller in 1991 than in 1981.
   2. The percentage was about the same.
   3. The percentage was larger in 1991 than in 1981.

10. To what extent have the following factors been considered when making enrollment decisions in the past ten years (1981-1991)?

	Not At All	To A Small Extent	To Some Extent	To A Great Extent	To A Very Great Extent
Demographic profiles of high school seniors within region of greatest employment	1	2	3	4	5
Market research studies of prospective student markets	1	2	3	4	5
Comparative profiles of enrolled freshmen with college-bound in-state freshmen	1	2	3	4	5
Summary reports of yield of enrolled students by characteristic and academic ability	1	2	3	4	5
Summary reports of undergraduate retention by student and program characteristic	1	2	3	4	5
Systematic procedures for monitoring freshmen persistence	1	2	3	4	5
Market research studies of currently enrolled student attitudes and perceptions	1	2	3	4	5

Survival Strategies for Christian Colleges and Universities

	Not At All	To A Small Extent	To Some Extent	To A Great Extent	To A Very Great Extent
Market research studies of withdrawn student attitudes and perceptions	1	2	3	4	5
Forecasts of course/staff requirements based on appropriate test populations and freshman course registration	1	2	3	4	5
Data provided by the College Board Enrollment Planning Service	1	2	3	4	5
Data provided by the ACT Enrollment Information Service	1	2	3	4	5

11. To what extent have the following activities been pursued by your college in the past ten years (1981-1991)?

	Not At All	To A Small Extent	To Some Extent	To A Great Extent	To A Very Great Extent
Annual evaluation of recruitment program	1	2	3	4	5
Annual evaluation of retention program	1	2	3	4	5
Increased emphasis on:					
early enrollment of high school students	1	2	3	4	5
special programs for high ability students	1	2	3	4	5
recruitment of part-time day students	1	2	3	4	5
recruitment of weekend students	1	2	3	4	5
recruitment of adult students	1	2	3	4	5
recruitment of minority students	1	2	3	4	5
recruitment of transfer students	1	2	3	4	5
recruitment of international students	1	2	3	4	5
special programs for business and industry	1	2	3	4	5
Visits to campus by prospective students and/or their families	1	2	3	4	5
Visits to campus by high school personnel (counselors, teachers, etc.)	1	2	3	4	5

	Not At All	To A Small Extent	To Some Extent	To A Great Extent	To A Very Great Extent
Visits to campus by church personnel (pastors, youth workers, youth groups, etc.)	1	2	3	4	5
High school visits by individual counselors	1	2	3	4	5
Home visits with prospective students and/or their families	1	2	3	4	5
Off-campus receptions, dinners for prospective students and/or their families	1	2	3	4	5
Participation in college nights, fairs, etc.	1	2	3	4	5
Displays, booths in central or public locations (malls, etc.)	1	2	3	4	5
Direct mailings to prospective students	1	2	3	4	5
Telephone calls by faculty to prospective students	1	2	3	4	5
Telephone calls by alumni to prospective students	1	2	3	4	5
Telephone calls by current students to prospective students	1	2	3	4	5
Toll free lines to the admissions office for prospective student use	1	2	3	4	5
Advertisements on/in:					
Billboards or transit bus/subways, etc.	1	2	3	4	5
Posters	1	2	3	4	5
Commercial radio or television	1	2	3	4	5
Public television	1	2	3	4	5
Local newspapers	1	2	3	4	5
High school newspapers	1	2	3	4	5
Magazines/journals	1	2	3	4	5
Promotional films, videotapes, cassettes, etc.	1	2	3	4	5
Utilization of the College Entrance Examination Board, ACT or other Student Searches/Mailing Lists	1	2	3	4	5

Survival Strategies for Christian Colleges and Universities

	Not At All	To A Small Extent	To Some Extent	To A Great Extent	To A Very Great Extent
Utilization of the following personnel in institutional recruitment activities:					
Faculty	1	2	3	4	5
Alumni	1	2	3	4	5
Current students	1	2	3	4	5
Coaches, other activity directors (e.g., band/choir directors, etc.)	1	2	3	4	5
Pastors	1	2	3	4	5
Administrators (non-admissions)	1	2	3	4	5
Trustees	1	2	3	4	5
Efforts to increase student employment on campus	1	2	3	4	5
Efforts to increase the number and/or amounts of financial aid awards	1	2	3	4	5
Use of financial aid to shape student body	1	2	3	4	5
An increase in the awarding of no-need merit scholarships	1	2	3	4	5
Summer orientation program for new students	1	2	3	4	5
Summer advising and registration for new students	1	2	3	4	5
Follow-up studies conducted with accepted students who fail to enroll (surveys, phone calls, etc.)	1	2	3	4	5
Follow-up studies conducted with prospects who fail to apply (surveys, phone calls, etc.)	1	2	3	4	5
Segmented orientation for student subgroups: (e.g., transfers, minorities, internationals, etc.)	1	2	3	4	5
Separate orientation program for parents	1	2	3	4	5
Communication with parents of prospective students (newsletter, brochure, special mailings, etc.)	1	2	3	4	5

	Not At All	To A Small Extent	To Some Extent	To A Great Extent	To A Very Great Extent
An administrator specifically responsible for monitoring attrition and developing retention programs	1	2	3	4	5
Attempts to increase student participation in student government, residence life and other campus activities	1	2	3	4	5
The development of a distinctive college character in comparison with competitors and/or other similar colleges	1	2	3	4	5
Targeted recruitment activities segmented by primary, secondary, and tertiary markets	1	2	3	4	5
Utilization of consultants to assist in recruitment and/or retention efforts	1	2	3	4	5
Development of formal, written recruitment plan	1	2	3	4	5
Development of formal, written retention plan	1	2	3	4	5

12. To what extent are the following statements characteristic of your college in the past ten years (1981-1991)?

	Not At All	To A Small Extent	To Some Extent	To A Great Extent	To A Very Great Extent
The mission statement is referred to for guidance in the development and implementation of enrollment programs	1	2	3	4	5
Enrollment concerns have become a priority across the campus	1	2	3	4	5
Necessary information for enrollment related decisions is readily available within this college	1	2	3	4	5
Formal lines of communication have been simplified to increase the flow of information among people in offices which influence enrollment	1	2	3	4	5

Survival Strategies for Christian Colleges and Universities

	To A Not At All	To Small Extent	To A Some Extent	To A Very Great Extent	Great Extent
Faculty and administrators demonstrate concern for the individual welfare of students and each other	1	2	3	4	5
This college places emphasis on serving students	1	2	3	4	5
The senior administration demonstrates concern for the individual welfare of students and each other	1	2	3	4	5
This campus is concerned with providing students with a high quality educational experience	1	2	3	4	5

13. To what do you attribute changes in the financial condition of your college during the ten year period 1981-1991?

Do you wish to receive a copy of the results of this study? Yes _____ No _____

Thank you very much for your assistance.

Institutional Code_____

STRATEGIC MANAGEMENT SURVEY

SECTION III: FINANCIAL MANAGEMENT

Please Note: An institutional code has been assigned to each institution and we are asking those who complete different sections of the survey to identify themselves. The code is used in order to match institutional responses with data which are being obtained from other sources as well as to ensure consistency in individual responses across institutions. However, <u>all information will remain confidential. No individual institution's response will be used. Only aggregate figures will be included in the write-up of this research project.</u>

Completed by: _____
Title: _____
Telephone Number: (____)_____ Extension:_____

Responses to this survey are based upon (please check all that apply):
_____ Your personal experience working at this college
       Please specify the number of years you have been at this college: _____
_____ Knowledge gained from sources other than your personal experience (i.e., other staff, faculty, historical data/reports, etc.)
_____ Other (please specify: _____)

Please rate your general level of awareness regarding the events which have transpired at your institution during the period 1981-1991: (please circle the appropriate numbers)

No Awareness		Somewhat Aware		Very Aware
1	2	3	4	5

<u>Instructions:</u> The following questions may be answered by filling in a blank or circling the appropriate number to designate your response. Feel free to make comments throughout the survey. There is an open-ended question at the end to provide you an opportunity to express your opinion and to make any additional comments not previously addressed in the survey. This survey should take no longer than 15 minutes to complete.

1. To what extent have the following activities been pursued by your college in the past ten years (1981-1991)?

	Not At All	To A Small Extent	To Some Extent	To A Great Extent	To A Very Great Extent
Reduction of academic programs through across-the-board cuts	1	2	3	4	5
Reduction of academic programs through selective cuts	1	2	3	4	5

Survival Strategies for Christian Colleges and Universities

	Not At All	To A Small Extent	To Some Extent	To A Great Extent	To A Very Great Extent
Reduction of non-academic programs through across-the-board cuts	1	2	3	4	5
Reduction of academic programs through selective cuts	1	2	3	4	5
Reduction of faculty size through natural attrition (death, retirement, etc.)	1	2	3	4	5
Reduction of professional staff through natural attrition (death, retirement, etc.)	1	2	3	4	5
Dismissal of non-tenured faculty in low student demand areas	1	2	3	4	5
Dismissal of tenured faculty in low student demand areas	1	2	3	4	5
Dismissal of non-tenured faculty in high student demand areas	1	2	3	4	5
Increasing academic fees (other than tuition)	1	2	3	4	5
Decreasing academic fees (other than tuition)	1	2	3	4	5
Decreasing non-academic fees	1	2	3	4	5
Increasing non-academic fees	1	2	3	4	5
Increasing tuition levels	1	2	3	4	5
Decreasing tuition levels	1	2	3	4	5
Faculty/staff salary reductions	1	2	3	4	5
Faculty/staff salary freeze	1	2	3	4	5
Deferring maintenance and repair funding	1	2	3	4	5
Decreasing equipment funding	1	2	3	4	5
Implementing energy-conservation programs	1	2	3	4	5
Development of contingency retrenchment plan	1	2	3	4	5

	Not At All	To A Small Extent	To Some Extent	To A Great Extent	To A Very Great Extent
Elimination of unprofitable academic programs	1	2	3	4	5
Elimination of unprofitable non-academic programs	1	2	3	4	5
Retraining faculty from low demand areas to high demand areas	1	2	3	4	5
Negotiation of early retirement with senior staff or faculty members	1	2	3	4	5
Merger of departments and programs	1	2	3	4	5
Merger of co-curricular services and programs	1	2	3	4	5
Development of cooperative arrangements with other institutions	1	2	3	4	5
Elimination of professional staff positions	1	2	3	4	5
Retraining faculty in low demand areas to fill staff positions	1	2	3	4	5
Implementation of tighter budget controls	1	2	3	4	5
Fundraising activities directed toward the following constituents:					
Alumni	1	2	3	4	5
Business and industry	1	2	3	4	5
Private foundations	1	2	3	4	5
Community organizations	1	2	3	4	5
Sponsoring denomination	1	2	3	4	5
Other religious organizations	1	2	3	4	5
Trustees	1	2	3	4	5
Fundraising activities in the following areas:					
Annual giving	1	2	3	4	5
Major gifts	1	2	3	4	5
Direct mail solicitation	1	2	3	4	5
Telephone solicitation	1	2	3	4	5
Capital Campaign	1	2	3	4	5
Use of marketing research to develop new sources of financial support	1	2	3	4	5

	Not At All	To A Small Extent	To Some Extent	To A Great Extent	To A Very Great Extent
Involvement of following personnel in fundraising activities:					
Alumni	1	2	3	4	5
Faculty	1	2	3	4	5
Trustees	1	2	3	4	5
Current students	1	2	3	4	5
Deliberate attempts to use gift money to reduce reliance on tuition income	1	2	3	4	5
Constructed or bought additional physical plant	1	2	3	4	5

2. To what extent are the following statements characteristic of your college in the past ten years (1981-1991)?

	Not At All	To A Small Extent	To Some Extent	To A Great Extent	To A Very Great Extent
The mission statement is referred to for guidance when making resource allocation decisions	1	2	3	4	5
Necessary information for financial decisions is readily available within this college	1	2	3	4	5
When cutbacks occur they are done on a prioritized basis	1	2	3	4	5
People at this college make resource decisions collegially	1	2	3	4	5
A rational process is used to make resource allocation decisions at this college	1	2	3	4	5
Resource allocation decisions are made bureaucratically at this college	1	2	3	4	5
Resource allocation decisions are made autocratically at this college	1	2	3	4	5
Persuasion, negotiation, and coalition-building are examples of what determines resource allocation	1	2	3	4	5

3. To what do you attribute changes in the financial condition of this college during the past ten years (1981-1991)?

Do you wish to receive a copy of the results of this study? Yes _____ No _____

Thank you very much for your assistance.

Institutional Code_____

STRATEGIC MANAGEMENT SURVEY

SECTION IV: PROGRAM DEVELOPMENT AND EXPANSION

Please Note: An institutional code has been assigned to each institution and we are asking those who complete different sections of the survey to identify themselves. The code is used in order to match institutional responses with data which are being obtained from other sources as well as to ensure consistency in individual responses across institutions. However, <u>all information will remain confidential. No individual institution's response will be used. Only aggregate figures will be included in the write-up of this research project.</u>

Completed by: _____
Title: _____
Telephone Number: (____)_____ Extension:_____

Responses to this survey are based upon (please check all that apply):
_____ Your personal experience working at this college
         Please specify the number of years you have been at this college: _____
_____ Knowledge gained from sources other than your personal experience (i.e., other staff, faculty, historical data/reports, etc.)
_____ Other (please specify: _____)

Please rate your general level of awareness regarding the events which have transpired at your institution during the period 1981-1991: (please circle the appropriate numbers)

No Awareness		Somewhat Aware		Very Aware
1	2	3	4	5

<u>Instructions</u>: The following questions may be answered by filling in a blank or circling the appropriate number to designate your response. Feel free to make comments throughout the survey. There is an open-ended question at the end to provide you an opportunity to express your opinion and to make any additional comments not previously addressed in the survey. This survey should take no longer than 15 minutes to complete.

1. How many full-time teaching faculty (excluding administrators and staff whose primary responsibility is non-classroom based) did your institution employ in <u>1991</u>?
   _____ (Estimate if necessary)

2. How many full-time teaching faculty (excluding administrators and staff whose primary responsibility is non-classroom based) did your institution employ in <u>1981</u>?

   _____ (Estimate if necessary)

3. How many <u>undergraduate</u> academic programs (i.e., majors, etc.) did your institution offer in <u>1991</u>?

   _____ (Estimate if necessary)

4. How many <u>graduate</u> academic programs did your institution offer in <u>1991</u>?
_____ (Estimate if necessary)

5. To what extent have the following activities been pursued by your college in the past ten years (1981-1991)?

	Not At All	To A Small Extent	To Some Extent	To A Great Extent	To A Very Great Extent
Addition of courses or programs in high student demand areas	1	2	3	4	5
Addition of courses in general education areas	1	2	3	4	5
Reallocation of funds to support innovative courses or programs	1	2	3	4	5
Reallocation of funds from low student demand area to high student demand area	1	2	3	4	5
Development of new on-campus programs to serve new clientele/ markets	1	2	3	4	5
Development of new off-campus programs to serve new clientele/ markets	1	2	3	4	5
Development of cooperative arrangements with other institutions to add academic programs or courses	1	2	3	4	5
Increased faculty teaching loads	1	2	3	4	5
Increased faculty/student ratio	1	2	3	4	5
Increased course section sizes	1	2	3	4	5
Enhanced faculty development program(s)	1	2	3	4	5
Expanded days and times when courses are offered	1	2	3	4	5
Added graduate level courses/ programs	1	2	3	4	5
Added required courses to curriculum	1	2	3	4	5
Created new majors through small changes in existing programs	1	2	3	4	5

Survival Strategies for Christian Colleges and Universities

	Not At All	To A Small Extent	To Some Extent	To A Great Extent	To A Very Great Extent
Added accelerated degree completion program(s)	1	2	3	4	5
Added new majors to meet emerging societal needs	1	2	3	4	5
Initiated truly innovative programs and courses	1	2	3	4	5
Strengthened academic support services	1	2	3	4	5
Use of part-time faculty in administrative positions	1	2	3	4	5
Added extended orientation program/course	1	2	3	4	5
Made changes to improve academic advising program/system	1	2	3	4	5
Made changes to improve career planning/placement programs	1	2	3	4	5
Made changes to improve religious life programs	1	2	3	4	5
Made changes to improve student development programs	1	2	3	4	5

6. To what extent are the following statements characteristic of your college in the past ten years (1981-1991)?

	Not At All	To A Small Extent	To Some Extent	To A Great Extent	To A Very Great Extent
The mission statement is referred to for guidance in the development and implementation of academic programs	1	2	3	4	5
Faculty/administrator cooperation is fostered	1	2	3	4	5
Necessary information for academic decision-making is readily available within this college	1	2	3	4	5
Graduate level courses/programs have changed the mission of this college	1	2	3	4	5

	To A Not At All	To Small Extent	To A Some Extent	To A Very Great Extent	Great Extent
This campus is concerned with providing students with a high quality educational experience	1	2	3	4	5
A new mission defines programs which are outside of faculty expertise	1	2	3	4	5
New undergraduate majors/programs have changed the mission of this college	1	2	3	4	5
Changes in required courses have changed the mission of this college	1	2	3	4	5
The faculty at this college are involved in ongoing program review and revision	1	2	3	4	5
Adversarial administrative/faculty relations exist at this college	1	2	3	4	5
Administration and faculty demonstrate increased sensitivity to market demands for relevant coursework	1	2	3	4	5
The academic programs offered here reflect the mission of the institution	1	2	3	4	5

7. To what do you attribute changes in the financial condition of this college during the ten year period 1981-1991?

Do you wish to receive a copy of the results of this study? Yes _____ No _____

Thank you very much for your assistance.

Appendix C

Operationalization of the Financial Condition Measures

The financial data for this study were obtained from the Higher Education General Information Survey (HEGIS), and the Integrated Postsecondary Education Data System Survey (IPEDS), conducted by the Department of Education's National Center for Education Statistics (NCES), and accessed through the NSF CASPAR System. From Fiscal Year (FY) 1966 (HEGIS I) through FY 1986 (HEGIS XXI), these data are derived from the annual Higher Education General Information Survey (HEGIS). Beginning in FY 1987 (IPEDS I), these data are derived from the new Integrated Postsecondary Education Data System Survey (IPEDS). FY 1987 is defined as the institutional fiscal year which ends in 1987. Data are current as of January 1991. The following section outlines the specific variables which comprise each ratio described in Chapter One. For each ratio, the percentage of change over time was calculated using each year of the ten-year period 1981-1991. In order to compensate for inflation, figures were put in 1991 dollars, using the Consumer Price Index for each year.

The ratios used to assess financial condition are defined and computed as follows:

Ratio 1. The Ratio of Total Assets to Total Liabilities

The first ratio provides a measure of an institution's overall financial strength. According to Prinvale (1992), "A high ratio indicates an institution has obtained a sufficient financial cushion to cover its long-term debts as well as to meet emergencies. A healthy endowment strengthens the asset side of the balance sheet, thus increasing this ratio" (p. 58). In fact, because of the importance of endowment for revenue generation, Standard and Poor (1990) takes into account both the endowment's absolute and relative size and its growth potential when assessing a college or university's financial flexibility. A positive percentage change in the ratio is the desired direction of change. Debt rating agencies typically stipulate that as long as debt is outstanding, available assets must be at least twice as great as general liabilities, making 2:1 the minimum threshold for this ratio (Rothschild, Unterberg, & Towbin, 1984).

1. Financial Assets - Sum of the following variables:

    A. <u>Total Endowment - Ending Market Value</u>
    Includes market value of gross investments of endowment, term endowment, and quasi-endowment (funds function as endowment) at the end of the fiscal year. If market value on some investments was not available, included whatever value was assigned by each institution in reporting market values in annual financial report.

B. Current Funds Balances - Ending

This variable represents the fund balance at the end of the fiscal year, after all additions, deductions, and transfers. The ending fund balance was computed as the difference between the beginning fund balance and the net increase or decrease.

2. Total Liabilities (Balance owed at end of year)

The amount shown in the liabilities section of the plan fund balance sheet for each institution at the end of the fiscal year. This included liability against auxiliary enterprise facilities as well as educational and general facilities. Examples of auxiliary enterprise facilities are those used for operation of housing, food service, book stores, and other units which are classified as auxiliary enterprises.

Ratio 2. The Ratio Of Endowment Income (Yield) To Total Educational And General Revenues

This ratio measures an institution's financial self-sufficiency. According to Massey (1990), "For many colleges, its endowment is the difference between survival and true vitality" (p. 103). All things being equal, a positive percentage change in the ratio is the desired direction of change. At the same time, it is important to look beyond just the directional change for this ratio. For instance, it is possible that this ratio could change because of an unplanned (and undesirable) decrease in revenues. A rising ratio of endowment income might also suggest that more endowment funds are available to invest, that improved investment performance has been achieved, or that new investment policies have been effective. In general, this ratio provides an important indicator over time of an institution's ability to attract resources and the ability of an institution's external environment to provide this support (Dickmeyer & Hughes, 1982).

1. Endowment Income

Includes the unrestricted income of endowment and similar funds, the restricted income of endowment and similar funds to the extent expended for current operating purposes, and income from funds held in trust by others under irrevocable trusts. For FY 1981-1987, the variable was defined as the sum of restricted endowment income and unrestricted endowment income.

2. Total Current Educational and General Revenues

Composed of all educational and general revenues including: tuition and fees, federal government grants, contracts, and appropriations; state and local governmental grants, contracts, and appropriations; private gifts, grants, and contracts; endowment income; sales and services of educational activities, and other items or revenues not covered elsewhere.

Ratio 3. The Ratio of Tuition and Fee Revenues to Total Educational and General Revenues

The institution's reliance on tuition and fees is a particularly important indicator of financial condition for private colleges. Prinvale (1992) suggest that "It is reasonable that the ratio of tuition and fee revenues to general educational revenues should be as low as possible and, when looking at trends, should be declining over time, as long as the decline is not due to unplanned enrollment decreases, inelasticity in tuition pricing, or inability to control the percentage of students on financial aid" (p. 59). However, if this ratio declines it should not be due to an influx of "soft" revenues (revenues whose attainment is beyond institutional control). Essentially, trends in this ratio indicate the institution's ability to continue drawing support from students (Dickmeyer & Hughes, 1982).

1. Student Tuition and Fee Revenues

    All tuition and fees assessed against students for current operating purposes.

2. Total Educational and General Revenues

    See ratio 2 above.

Ratio 4. The Ratio of Unrestricted Funds Balances to Total Expenditures and Mandatory Transfers

This ratio is a general measure of an "institution's liquidity" (Prinvale, 1992) and provides an indication of how much money is immediately available for meeting unexpected demands. In other words, this ratio provides a sense of how much "cushion" a college has for meeting its obligations. A declining ratio is a warning that expenses may be outpacing revenues (Rothschild, Unterberg, & Towbin, 1984). As with ratios 1 and 2, a positive percentage change in the ratio is the desired direction of change.

1. Unrestricted Current Funds Balances - Ending

    This variable represents the fund balance at the end of the fiscal year, after all additions, deductions, and transfers. The ending fund balance was computed as the difference between the beginning fund balance and the net increase/decrease.

2. Total Expenditures and Mandatory Transfers

    This variable is composed of all expenditures and mandatory transfers as reported on each institution's Statement of Current Funds Revenues, Expenditures, and Other Changes. Both unrestricted and restricted amounts are included, whereas nonmandatory transfers are excluded.

Ratio 5. The Ratio of Net Revenues to Total Revenues

This ratio indicates whether total current operations for a given year resulted in a surplus or a deficit. This ratio is one of the primary indicators of the underlying causes of an institution's financial condition and provides an answer to the question, Did the institution live within its means during the year being reported on? A positive ratio indicates a surplus for the year reported on. In general, the larger the surplus, the stronger the institution's financial condition as a result of the year's operation. A negative ratio indicates a deficit for the year. A strong pattern of large deficits occurring in successive years is a strong warning signal that the institution is in a seriously weakened financial condition. As with ratios 1, 2, and 4, a positive percentage change in the ratio is the desired direction of change.

1. Net Revenues

    This variable is composed of all current funds (unrestricted and restricted) revenues less all current funds expenditures and mandatory transfers.

2. Total Revenues

    This variable is composed of all current funds revenues (including both unrestricted and restricted funds).

Ratio 6. Ratio of Opening Fall FTE Enrollment in 1991 to Opening Fall FTE Enrollment in 1981

This ratio is important because a primary purpose for colleges and universities is to serve students. Total enrollment is a crucial element in assessing the financial viability of most colleges and universities. Creditors often focus on data such as total enrollment as well as enrollment components (i.e., full-time, part-time, resident, non-resident) in addition to looking at trends and patterns in enrollment over time (Rothschild, Unterberg, & Towbin, 1984). This ratio is particularly important for small, private colleges which derive a substantial share of their revenue base from tuition and fees. A positive or stable percentage change is the desired direction for this ratio unless the institution has intentionally capped its enrollments or made a decision to reduce its enrollments.

1. Opening Fall FTE Enrollment in 1991

    This variable refers to the "full-time equivalent" enrollment at each institution as reported for Fall 1991. FTE enrollment equals the sum of the total number of full-time students plus one-third of the total number of part time students.

2. Opening Fall FTE Enrollment in 1981

    This variable refers to the "full-time equivalent" enrollment at each institution as reported for Fall 1981. FTE enrollment equals the sum of the total number of full-time students plus one-third of the total number of part-time students.

References

AACRAO. (1986). *Demographics, standards and equity: Challenges in college admissions.* New York: College Board Publications.

Aldrich, H. (1979). *Organizations and environments.* Englewood Cliffs, N.J.: Prentice-Hall.

Aldrich, H., & Pfeffer, J. (1976). Environments of organizations. *Annual Review of Sociology, 2,* 79-105.

Alexander, S. (1990, June 8). Colleges find fewer freshmen to go around. *The Wall Street Journal,* p. B1.

Almanac issue. (1993, August). The Chronicle of Higher Education.

The American Council on Education. (1993). *Campus trends, 1993.* Washington, D.C.: The American Council on Education.

The American Council on Education. (1994). Campus trends, *1994.* Washington, D.C.: The American Council on Education.

The American Council on Education. (1995). Campus trends, *1995.* Washington, D.C.: The American Council on Education.

Anderson, R.E. (1978). A financial and environmental analysis of strategic policy change at small private colleges. *Journal of Higher Education, 49,* 30-46.

Anderson, R.E. (1975). *Finance and effectiveness: A study of college environments.* Princeton, N.J.: Educational Testing Service.

Ansoff, H.I., & Hayes, R.L. (1976). Introduction. In H.I. Ansoff, R.P. Declerck, & R.L. Hayes (Eds.), *From strategic planning to strategic management* (pp. 1-12). New York: Wiley.

Astin, A.W., & Lee, C.B. (1972). *The invisible colleges: A profile of small, private colleges with limited resources.* New York: McGraw-Hill Book Company.

Astin, A.W., Korn, W.S., & Berz, E.R. (1990). *The American freshman: National norms for fall 1990.* Los Angeles: University of California, Higher Education Research Institute.

Bakke, R. (1987). *The urban Christian.* Downers Grove, Il.: Inter-Varsity Press.

Baldridge, J.V., Kemerer, F.R., & Green, K.C. (1982). *The enrollment crisis: Factors, actors, and impacts.* (AAHE-ERIC/Higher Education Research Report, No. 3). Washington, D.C.: American Association for Higher Education.

Bean, J.P. (1983). Interaction effects based on class level in an exploratory model of college student dropout syndrome. Paper presented at annual meeting of American Education Research Association, Montreal, Canada, April 1983.

Birnbaum, R. (1983). *Maintaining diversity in American higher education.* San Francisco: Jossey-Bass.

Boulding, K.E. (1975). The management of decline. *Change,7*(5), 8-9.

Bowen, H.R., & Glenny, L.A. (1980). *Uncertainty in public higher education: Response to stress in ten California colleges and universities.* Sacramento, CA: California Postsecondary Education Committee.

Brazziel, W.F. (1985). Correlates of enrollment maintenance in liberal arts colleges. *College and University, 60*(2), 151-154.

Breland, H.M., Wilder, G., & Robertson, N.J. (1986). *Demographics, standards, and equity: Challenges in college admissions.* Iowa City, IA: The American College Testing Program.

Breneman, D.W. (1982). *The coming enrollment crisis: What every trustee must know.* Washington, D.C.: The Association of Governing Boards of Universities and Colleges.

Breneman, D.W., & Finn, C.E. (1978). An uncertain future. In D.W. Breneman, & C.E. Finn, Jr. (Eds.), *Public policy and private higher education* (pp. 1-61). Washington, D.C.: The Brookings Institute.

Buffington, S.P. (1990). Small liberal arts colleges: Strategies which lead to enrollment success (Doctoral Dissertation, Indiana University, 1990). *Dissertation Abstracts International, 51/10,* 3279.

Cameron, K.S. (1983). Strategic responses to conditions of decline: Higher education and the private sector. *Journal of Higher Education, 54*(4), 359-390.

Cameron, K.S. (1984). Organizational adaptation and higher education. *Journal of Higher Education, 55*(2), 122-144.

Cameron, K.S., & Whetten, D.A. (1981). Perceptions of organizational effectiveness over organizational life cycles. *Administrative Science Quarterly, 26,* 525-544.

Campolo, T. (1994). *Wake up America! Answering God's radical call while living in the real world.* San Francisco: Zondervan.

The Carnegie Foundation for the Advancement of Teaching. (1975). *More than survival: Prospects for higher education in a period of uncertainty.* San Francisco, CA.: Jossey-Bass.

The Carnegie Council on Policy Studies in Higher Education.(1980). *Three thousand futures: The next twenty years for higher education.* San Francisco: Jossey-Bass.

Carter, C.M. (1985). Adaptive and interpretive recruitment strategies of five small, liberal arts colleges (Doctoral Dissertation, University of North Carolina at Greensboro, 1985). *Dissertation Abstracts International, 46/11,* 3201.

Centra, J.A. (1978). *College enrollment in the 1980's: Projections and possibilities.* New York: College Entrance Examination Board.

Chabotar, K.J., & Honan, J.P. (1990). Coping with retrenchment: Strategies and tactics. *Change, 22*(6), 28-39.

Chaffee, E.E. (1984). Successful strategic management in small private colleges. *Journal of Higher Education, 55*(2),212-241.

Chaffee, E.E. (1985a). The concept of strategy: From business to higher education. In J.C. Smart (Ed.), *Higher education: Handbook of theory and research* (pp. 133-172). New York: Agathon Press, Inc.

Chaffee, E.E. (1985b). Three models of strategy. *Academy of Management Review, 10*(1), 89-98.

Chaffee, E.E., & Tierney, W.G. (1988). *Collegiate culture and leadership strategies.* New York: American Council on Education and Macmillian Publishing Co.

Chandler, A.D. (1962). *Strategy and structure: Chapters in the history of the industrial enterprise.* Cambridge, MA.: M.I.T. Press.

Christian College Coalition. (1986). [Final fall 1985 enrollment/application survey]. Duplicated material.

Child, J. (1972). Organizational structure, environment, and performance: The role of strategic choice. *Sociology, 6,* 35-44.

Choose a Christian college. (1994). Princeton, NJ: Peterson's Guides and the Christian College Coalition.

Clark, B.R. (1970). *The distinctive colleges.* Chicago: Aldine.

Clark, S.A. (Ed.). (1989, April). *A comparative general study of member institutions of the Christian college coalition.* (Available from [The Christian College Coalition, Washington, DC]).

Cohen, B.G. (1983). An analysis of institutional response and environmental constraints with respect to patterns of institutional enrollment decline in American higher education. Paper presented at the Association for the Study of Higher Education Conference, Washington, D.C., March.

Collier, D.J. (1982). Making financial assessments more meaningful. In C. Frances (Ed.), *New directions for higher education: Successful responses to financial difficulty* (No. 38. pp. 85-94). San Francisco: Jossey-Bass.

Collins, J.C., & Porras, J.I. (1994). *Built to last: Successful habits of visionary companies.* New York: Harper Collins Publishers.

Cope, R.G. (1981). *Strategic planning, management and decision making.* Washington, D.C.: American Association of Higher Education.

Crockett, D.S. (1985). Academic advising. In L. Noel, R. Levitz, D. Saluri & Associates (Eds.), *Increasing student retention* (pp. 244-263). San Francisco: Jossey-Bass.

Crossland, F.E. (1980). Learning to cope with the downward slope. *Change, 12*(5), 18, 20-25.

Cyert, R. (1980). The management of universities of constant or decreasing size. In *Current issues in higher education —Strategies for retrenchment: National, state, or institutional, 2*(6), 38-46. American Association for Higher Education.

David, R.M. (Ed.). (1985). *Leadership and institutional renewal.* New Directions for Higher Education, No. 49. San Francisco: Jossey-Bass.

DeLoughry, T.J. (1991, May 8). In Washington, outlook for colleges worsen as bad publicity abound. *The Chronicle of Higher Education, 37*(34), A1, A26-27.

Dickmeyer, N., & Hughes, K.S. (1982). Financial self-assessment. In C. Frances (Ed.), *New directions for higher education: Successful responses to financial difficulty,* (No. 38. pp. 19-25) San Francisco: Jossey-Bass.

Drucker, P. (1980). *Managing in turbulent times.* New York: Harper & Row.

Engel, J. (1983). *Averting the financial crisis in Christian organizations: Insights from a decade of donor research.* Wheaton, IL: Management Development Associates.

Enrollment Management Consultants. (1987). *Highlights of attitudinal studies of prospects, inquiries, non-matriculants, and matriculants.* Washington, D.C.: The Christian College Coalition.

Erekson, O.H. (1986). Revenue sources in higher education: Trends and analysis. In M.P. McKeown & K. Alexander (Eds.), *Values in conflict: Funding priorities in higher education* (pp. 41-62). Cambridge, MA: Ballinger.

Fadil, V.A., & Carter, N.A. (1980). *Openings, closings, mergers, and accreditation status of independent colleges and universities: Winter 1970 through summer 1979.* Washington, D.C.: National Institute of Independent Colleges and Universities.

Finkelstein, M.J., Farrar, D., & Pfinster, A.D. (1984). The adaptation of liberal arts colleges to the 1970s: An analysis of critical events. *Journal of Higher Education, 55*(2), 242-268.

Fischer, F.J. (1990). State financing of higher education: A new look at an old problem. *Change, 22*(1), 42-56.

Frances, C. (1986). Changing enrollment trends: Implications for the future financing of higher education. In M.P. McKeown & K. Alexander (Eds.), *Values in conflict: Funding priorities in higher education* (pp. 23-40). Cambridge, MA: Ballinger.

Frances, C., Huxel, G., Meyerson, J., & Park, D. (1987). *Strategic decision making: Key questions and indicators for trustees.* Washington, DC: Association of Governing Boards of Universities and Colleges.

Galbraith, J.R. (1977). *Organizational design.* Reading MA: Addison-Wesley.

Gerald, D.E., & Hussar, W.J. (1991). *Projections of education statistics to 2002.* Washington, D.C.: National Center for Education Statistics.

Ginter, P.M., & White, D.D. (1982). A social learning approach to strategic management: Toward a theoretical foundation. *Academy of Management Review, 7,* 253-261.

Glenny, L.A., Shea, J.R., Ruyle, J.H., & Freschi, K.H. (1976). *Presidents confront reality: From edifice complex to university without walls.* San Francisco: Jossey-Bass.

Grassmuck, K. (1990, November 14). Fewer students from middle class enrolling in college. *The Chronicle of Higher Education, 37*(11), A1, A40.

Green, J.S., & Levine, A. (1985). *Opportunity in adversity.* San Francisco: Jossey-Bass.

Hambrick, D.C. (1982). Environmental scanning and organizational strategy. *Strategic Management Journal, 3,* 159-174.

Hambrick, D.C., & Schechter, S.M. (1983). Turnaround strategies for mature industrial-product business units. *Academy of Management Journal, 25,* 510-531.

Hamlin, A., & Hungerford, C. (1988-89). How private colleges survive a financial crisis: Tools for effective planning and management. *Planning for Higher Education, 17*(2), 29-38.

Hammond, M.F. (1984, May/June). Survival of small, private colleges. *Journal of Higher Education, 55*(3), 360-388.

Hannan, M.T., & Freeman, J. (1977). The population ecology of organizations. *American Journal of Sociology, 82,* 929-964.

Harrington, P., & Sum, A. (1988, September/October). Whatever happened to the college enrollment crisis? *Academe,* 17-22.

Hartman, R.W. (1978). Federal options for student aid. In D.W. Breneman, & C.E. Finn, Jr. (Eds.), *Public policy and private higher education* (pp. 231-280). Washington, DC: The Brookings Institute.

Hauptman, A.M. (1990). *The tuition dilemma: Assessing new ways to pay for college.* Washington, DC: The Brookings Institute.

Hedberg, B., Nystrom, P., & Starbuck, W. (1976). Camping on seesaws: Prescriptions for a self-designing organization. *Administrative Science Quarterly, 21*, 41-65.

Hilpert, J.M. (1985). Enrollment success in private postsecondary institutions (Doctoral Dissertation, University of Michigan, 1985). *Dissertation Abstracts International, 46/11*, 3263.

Hilpert, J.M. (1987). Enrollment success in private colleges and universities. Paper presented at a meeting of the Association for the Study of Higher Education, San Diego, February.

Hofer, C.F. (1980). Turnaround strategies. *Journal of Business Strategy, 1*, 19-31.

Hollander, E. (1958). Conformity status and idiosyncrasy credit. *Psychological Review, 65*, 117-127.

Hossler, D. (1984). *Enrollment management: An integrated approach*. New York: College Entrance Examination Board.

Hossler, D. (1986). *Managing college enrollments*. New Directions for Higher Education, No. 53. San Francisco: Jossey-Bass.

Hossler, D. (1990). *The strategic management of college enrollments*. San Francisco: Jossey-Bass.

Hubbard, D.L. (1985). The seven commandments: Hallmarks of the successful church-related college. *Case Currents, November/December*, 12-15.

Hughes, K., Frances, C., & Lombardo, B. (1991). *Years of challenge: The impact of demographic and work force trends on higher education in the 1990s*. Washington, D.C.

Jonsen, R.W. (1984). Small colleges cope with the eighties: Sharp eye on the horizon, strong hand on the tiller. *Journal of Higher Education, 55*(2), 171-183.

Keller, G. (1983). *Academic strategy: The management revolution in American higher education*. Baltimore: Johns Hopkins University Press.

Kemerer, F.R., Baldridge, J.V., & Green, K.C. (1982). *Strategies for effective enrollment management*. Washington, D.C.: American Association of State Colleges and Universities.

Kerr, C. (1990). *The preservation of excellence in American higher education: The essential role of private colleges and universities*. Denver, Co.: The Education Commission of the States Task Force on State Policy and Independent Higher Education.

King, R.A. (1981). *The crisis in higher education: Facing reduction and financial exigency*. (Report No. HE 014-246). Albuquerque, N.M.: University of New Mexico, Department of Educational Administration. (ERIC Document Reproduction Service No. ED 206 225).

Kotler, P., & Murphy, P.E. (1981). Strategic planning for higher education. *Journal of Higher Education, 52*(5), 470-489.

Lapovsky, L., & Allard, S. (1986). State support for higher education. In M.P. McKeown & K. Alexander (Eds.), *Values in conflict: Funding priorities in higher education* (pp. 91-112). Cambridge, MA: Ballinger.

Levitz, R. & Noel, L. (1995). The earth-shaking but quiet revolution in retention management. Paper presented at the national conference on student retention, New York City, New York, August 1995.

Martin, W.B. (1984). Adaptation and distinctiveness. *Journal of Higher Education, 55*(2), 286-296.

McKelvey, W. (1982). *Organizational systematics: Taxonomy, evolution, and classification.* Berkeley: University of California Press.

McMillen, L. (1991, February 13). Cut staffs but not across the board, strapped colleges are advised. *The Chronicle of Higher Education, 37*(22), A31, A34.

McPherson, M.S. (1978). The demand for higher education. In D.W. Breneman, & C.E. Finn, Jr. (Eds.), *Public policy and private higher education* (pp. 143-196). Washington, DC: The Brookings Institute.

Mayhew, L.B. (1979). *Surviving the eighties: Strategies and procedures for solving fiscal and enrollment problems.* San Francisco: Jossey-Bass.

Miles, R.E., & Snow, C.C. (1978). *Organizational strategy, structure, and process.* New York: McGraw-Hill.

Miles, R.H., & Cameron, K.S. (1982). *Coffin nails and corporate strategies.* Englewood Cliff, N.J.: Prentice-Hall.

Miller, D., & Friesen, P.H. (1980). Archetypes of organizational transition. *Administrative Science Quarterly, 25,* 268-99.

Millet, J.D. (1977). *Managing turbulence and change.* San Francisco: Jossey-Bass.

Mingle, J.R., & Norris, D.M. (1981). Institutional strategies for responding to decline. In J.R. Mingle & Associates (Eds.), *Challenges of retrenchment.* San Francisco: Jossey-Bass.

Minter, W.J. (1978). *Independent higher education.* Washington, D.C. : National Association of Independent Colleges and Universities.

Minter, W.J., & Bowen, H.R. (1977). *Private higher education.* Washington, D.C.: Association of American Colleges.

Minter, W.J., Hughes, K.S., Robinson, D.D., Turk, F.J., Buchanan, A.D. & Prager, F.J. (1982). *Ratio analysis in higher education.* New York: Peat, Marwick, Mitchell, and Co., & L.F. Rothschild, Unterberg, Towbin.

Minter, W.J., Prager, F.J., Hughes, K.S., Robinson, D.D. & Turk, F.J. (1982). Using ratio analysis to evaluate financial performance. In C. Frances (Ed.), *New directions for higher education: Successful responses to financial difficulty.* (pp. 25-36). San Francisco, CA.: Jossey-Bass.

Mintzberg, H. (1978). Patterns in strategy formation. *Management Science, 24,* 934-948.

Mintzberg, H., & Waters, J.A. (1982). Tracking strategy in an entrepreneurial firm. *Academy of Management Journal, 25,* 465-499.

Mooney, C.J. (1989, January 18). Aggressive marketing and recruiting bring a renaissance to some private colleges. *The Chronicle of Higher Education, 35,* A13.

Morriss-Olson, M. (1995). An investigation into the management strategies employed and the financial conditions obtained by member institutions of the Coalition for Christian Colleges & Universities from 1981 to 1991 (Doctoral Dissertation, Loyola University, 1995).

Mosely, J.D., & Bucher, G.R. (1982). Church-related colleges in a changing context. *Educational Record, 63,* 46-51.

Muston, R. (1985). *Marketing and enrollment management in state universities*. Iowa City, IA: The American College Testing Program.

Nelson, S.C. (1978). Financial trends and issues. In D.W. Breneman, & C.E. Finn, Jr. (Eds.), *Public policy and private higher education* (pp. 63-142). Washington, DC: The Brookings Institute.

O'Keefe, M. (1985). Whatever happened to the crash of '80,'81, '82, '83, '84, and '85? *Change*, May/June, 37-41.

O'Keefe, M. (1989). Private colleges: Beating the odds. *Change, 21*(10), 10.

Paine, F.T., & Anderson, C.R. (1977). Contingencies affecting strategy formulation and effectiveness: An empirical study. *Journal of Management Studies, 14*, 147-158.

Parker, B. (1987). Predictors of turnaround: What really matters? Unpublished manuscript.

Peat, Marwick, Mitchell and Co., & Rothschild, Unterberg, Towbin (1984). *Ratio analysis in higher education: A guide to assessing the institutional financial condition*. (2nd ed.). New York: Peat, Marwick, Mitchell and Co., & Rothschild, Unterberg, Towbin.

Peck, R.D. (1984). Entrepreneurship as a significant factor in successful adaptation. *Journal of Higher Education, 55*(2), 212-241.

Perkins, J. (1993). *Beyond charity: The call to Christian community development*. Grand Rapids, Mi.: Baker Books.

Peters, T. (1994). *The Tom Peters seminar: Crazy times for crazy organizations*. New York: Random House, Inc.

Peters, T.J., & Waterman, R.H. (1982). *In search of excellence*. New York: Harper and Row.

Peterson, M.W. (1980). Analyzing alternative approaches to planning. In P. Jedamus & M.W. Peterson & Associates (Eds.), *Improving Academic Management*. San Francisco: Jossey-Bass.

Pfeffer, J., & Salancik, G.R. (1978). *The external control of organizations*. New York: Harper and Row.

Pfinster, A.O., Finkelstein, M., Gordon, W., & Farrar, D. (1982). Change and continuity in the undergraduate college: Adaptation and its consequences. Paper presented at the annual meeting of the Association for the Study of Higher Education, Washington, D.C.

Prinvale, J.M. (1992). What happens when colleges plan? The use of strategic planning in four-year colleges and universities (Doctoral Dissertation, Stanford University, 1992). *Dissertation Abstracts International, 53/09*, 3122.

Quinn, R.E., & Cameron, K.S. (1983). Organizational life cycles and shifting criteria of effectiveness: Some preliminary evidence. *Management Science, 29*, 33-51.

Ringenberg, W.C. (1984). *The Christian college: A history of protestant higher education in America*. Grand Rapids, MI: William B. Eerdmans Publishing Co.

Rothenburg, A. (1979). *The emerging goddess*. Chicago: University of Chicago Press.

Rubin, I.S. (1979). Retrenchment, loose structure and adaptability in the University. *Social Science Quarterly, 58*, 242-254.

St. John, E.P. (1991). The transformation of private liberal arts colleges. *The Review of Higher Education, 15*, 83-106.

Sandin, R.T. (1982). *The search for excellence: The Christian college in an age of competition.* Macon, Ga: Mercer University Press.

Sandin, R.T. (1992). To those who teach at Christian colleges. In D.S. Guthrie & R.L. Noftzger, Jr. (Eds.), *Agenda for church-related colleges and universities* (pp. 43-55). New Directions for Higher Education, No. 79. San Francisco: Jossey-Bass.

Scarlett, M. (1982). Survival gear for the small college. *AGB Reports*, January/February, 22-27.

Shirley, R.C. (1982). Limiting the scope of strategy: A decision-based approach. *Academy of Management Review, 7,* 262-268.

Smart, J.C. (1989). Organizational decline and effectiveness in higher education. *Research in Higher Education, 30,* 387-401.

Smith, J., & Finch, H.L. (1975). Private colleges: Strategies for change. *Planning for Higher Education, 4,* 3-4.

Snow, C.C., & Hrebiniak, L.G. (1980). Strategy, distinctiveness, competence, and organizational performance. *Administrative Science Quarterly, 25,* 317-35.

Stadtman, V.A. (1980). *Academic adaptation: Higher education prepares for the 1980's and 1990's.* San Francisco: Jossey-Bass.

Steeples, D.W. (Ed.). (1986). *Institutional revival: Case histories.* New Directions for Higher Education, No. 54. San Francisco: Jossey-Bass.

Tempel, E.R. (1985). Organizational response to scarcity in small colleges: The impact of leader behavior and faculty influence in decision making (Doctoral Dissertation, Indiana University, 1985). *Dissertation Abstracts International, 46/07,* 1851.

Tierney, W.G. (1989). Symbolism and presidential perceptions of leadership. *Review of Higher Education, 12*(2), 153-166.

Tierney, W.G. (1988). Organizational culture in higher education: Defining the essentials. *Journal of Higher Education, 59*(1), 2-21.

U.S. Department of Education. (1992a). *Digest of educational statistics, 1992.* Washington, DC: Office of Educational Research and Improvement.

U.S. Department of Education. (1993a). *Digest of educational statistics, 1993.* Washington, DC: Office of Educational Research and Improvement.

U.S. Department of Education. (1992b). *The condition of education, 1992.* Washington, DC: National Center for Education Statistics.

U.S. Department of Education. (1993b). *The condition of education, 1993.* Washington, DC: National Center for Education Statistics.

Voluntary Support of Education, 1987-88. (1989). New York, NY: Council for Aid to Education, Inc.

Wamsley, G., & Zald, M. (1973). *The political economy of public organizations.* Lexington, Mass.: D.C. Heath.

Weick, K.E. (1976). Educational organizations as loosely coupled systems. *Administrative science quarterly, 21,* 1-19.

West, D.C. (1982). How endangered are small colleges? *Educational Record, 63*(4), 14-17.

Western Interstate Commission for Higher Education. (1992). *High school graduates: Projections by state, 1992-2009.* Boulder, CO: Western Interstate Commission for Higher Education, The College Board, and Teachers Insurance and Annuity Association.

Whetten, D.A., & Cameron, K.S. (1985). Administrative effectiveness in higher education. *Review of Higher Education, 9*(1), 35-49.

Wilmer, W.K. (1990). *Friends, funds, and freshmen.* Washington, D.C.: Christian College Coalition.

Zammuto, R.F. (1983). Growth, stability, and decline in American college and university enrollments. *Educational Administration Quarterly, 19*(1), 83-89.

Zammuto, R.F. (1984). Are the liberal arts an endangered species? *Journal of Higher Education, 55*, 184-211.

Zammuto, R.F. (1986). Managing decline in American higher education. In J.C. Smart (Ed.), *Higher Education: Handbook of Theory and Research.* (Vol. 2, pp. 43-84). New York: Agathon.